Becoming Celestial Soul Mates

10 GOLDEN RULES FOR A RICHER RELATIONSHIP

Becoming
Celestial Soul Mates

10 Golden Rules for a Richer Relationship

Trafford R. Cole, PsyD

CFI
Springville, Utah

ISBN 13: 978-1-55517-954-0
ISBN 10: 1-55517-954-1

Published by CFI, an imprint of Cedar Fort, Inc., 2373 W. 700 S., Springville, UT, 84663
Distributed by Cedar Fort, Inc., www.cedarfort.com

LIBRARY OF CONGRESS CATALOGING-IN-PUBLICATION DATA
    Library of Congress Cataloging-in-Publication Data

    Cole, Trafford R. (Trafford Robertson), 1951-
      Celestial soul mates : ten golden rules for a richer relationship / by Trafford R. Cole.
        p. cm.
      Includes index.
      ISBN 1-55517-954-1
      1. Marriage—Mormon authors. 2. Man-woman relationships—Religious aspects—Christianity.
    I. Title.

      BX8641.C65 2006
      248.8'44—dc22

                                    2006022804

Cover design by Nicole Williams
Cover design © 2006 by Lyle Mortimer
Typeset by Annaliese B. Cox

Printed in the United States of America

10 9 8 7 6 5 4 3 2 1

Printed on acid-free paper

Dedication

To Fernanda, my wife, eternal companion, and soul mate,
who has taught me these principles through her example and love.
This book contains those principles that I am striving to master, and I
ask your forgiveness for the times I fall short of these ideals.

Table of Contents

Introduction

My beloved is mine, and I am his.

—The Song of Solomon 2:16

For centuries, the above verse has been engraved in Hebrew on the wedding bands of Jewish husbands and wives. Does it describe your marriage?

Several years ago, when my wife and I celebrated our silver wedding anniversary, we asked ourselves, "Why has our marriage worked out so well? Were we just lucky? Did we somehow find the perfect match?"

As we look back over the years, however, we find that we had many difficulties, the same that are often cited as causes of divorce. We have had financial difficulties, sexual problems, misunderstandings with in-laws, differences in our perceptions about politics, challenges with child rearing, struggles with our careers, and just about everything I can imagine.

We did not come from perfect families with good role models. My parents separated when I was ten after intense conflict and divorced two years later. My sheltered world collapsed. My wife's father abandoned her mother before she was born, and her mother struggled to support her and bring her up. The first and only thing we agreed on when we first met was that we would never get married. Yet we did, we are together, we love each other, and we are looking forward to another twenty or thirty years together here on earth and an eternity together if we are faithful enough to earn it. As Latter-day Saints, we expect much more from marriage than just feeling better, or getting along. Listen to the promise of the Lord:

> And again, verily I say unto you, if a man marry a wife by my word, which is my law, and by the new and everlasting covenant, and it is sealed unto them by the Holy Spirit of Promise, by him who is anointed. . . . Ye shall come forth in the first resurrection; . . . and shall inherit thrones, kingdoms, principalities, and powers, dominions, all heights and depths. . . . Then they shall

be gods, because they have no end; therefore shall they be from everlasting to everlasting, because they continue; then shall they be above all, because all things are subject unto them. Then shall they be gods, because they have all power, and the angels are subject unto them. (D&C 132:19–20)

Can you envision a husband and wife fulfilling this promise by just getting along, or must the relationship become far more profound and intimate? Can we inherit all this if we don't become celestial soul mates?

This book asks: What is necessary to become and remain soul mates and intimate friends for this life and for all eternity? How can we become celestial soul mates? What is the difference between just being married and having a deeper relationship as soul mates? Is this possible in mortal life? Does it just happen, or are there ways to become soul mates? If so, what are the steps we have to take? This book attempts to give some answers.

Most marriage manuals focus on helping couples with difficulties. While that is good, I see a need to give suggestions on how to prevent the most common problems in marriage *before* they surface. Why do most couples have problems communicating or finding solutions to their problems? We need to find ways to enrich and deepen the roots of the relationship before the problems arise, and thus allow the couple to withstand the winds of adversity and the storms of life so that the relationship continues to flourish and grow.

These suggestions are not based only on my personal experience. By examining my own marriage, however, I have learned principles and rules that allow a relationship to grow, flourish, and develop, rather than to shrivel and die.

As a marriage counselor, I have been struck by how often couples come into therapy with the same problems as so many others. I also find these same patterns repeated in the professional literature of marital therapy. Each couple has their individual variation, but at the root, we often find the same complaints, misunderstandings, unrealistic expectations, and warped perceptions. In addition, when we address these aspects and provide some relationship skills, we often see understanding and appreciation replace the fighting and bitterness.

As a university professor of adult education classes such as Human Sexuality and The Psychology of Interpersonal Relations, I have had the rare privilege of examining the experiences of hundreds of married and single students. One of my favorite exercises has always been to divide the class into groups and ask each group to come up with "ten golden rules for a successful relationship." Their considerations have been instrumental in forming these concepts.

As these ideas have taken form, they have become the basis of the marital enrichment seminars I have taught for the Army Family Advocacy program, church groups, and conferences of interested couples. Often the most significant part of these discussions is for each person to discover that he or she is not the only one with that problem.

Discovering that many husbands besides yours clam up emotionally is comforting. It takes on added meaning to understand that men and women think and react differently on an emotional level for biological and physiological reasons. When men find out why women are so sensitive to nonverbal cues like tone of voice and facial expressions, it opens up new insight into the female's perception of the world. When this understanding occurs, we begin to appreciate and value the differences.

This work is the compilation of many different experiences and intends to offer insight into those aspects of intimate interaction that are essential to a long-lasting and fulfilling relationship. Over the years, I have collected eighty-eight different golden rules. The difficulty has been to condense these down to something not only manageable but something that renders the essence of what is needed for a good relationship.

The following are ten principles that should govern our *actions* in a relationship. These are not just theories or concepts but essential principles. Without one or more of these, the relationship will suffer. I believe that it is necessary for every couple to develop these traits, behaviors, and perceptions so that their marriage is an experience of growth and satisfaction.

This book is specifically written for the LDS member who already believes in the value of eternal marriage, but it can be useful to anyone who cares about his or her relationship. The principles of creating deep, intimate relationships are universal and apply to all couples. This book assumes that the couples are already living the principles of the gospel. Seeking the spirit through daily prayer and study of the word of God, and obedience to the commandments of the Lord are essential elements of any celestial marriage. Because these principles are constantly illustrated through the talks of our church leaders and many books, this work does not dwell on them. Rather it desires to provide additional principles of relationships that might not be so obvious or so well known.

No one comes into life or into the relationship a master of all of these principles. In fact, it is having an intimate relationship that allows many of these to develop. What is important is that the couple works together so that each person can grow and better express their love. A relationship is a growing experience and is more fulfilling and rewarding the longer it grows.

Contrary to common opinion, marriage should improve as the years go by. Intimacy should increase, and the love and joy of being together should be stronger at the end of life than when newly married. If your honeymoon was the best time of your life together, something is wrong. Often patience is needed. An oak tree does not grow overnight. We need to exercise patience with ourselves and with our spouse. Thus, *soul mates* are made, not found. We first connect on some level, but then we can and should deepen this connection throughout life, not merely assume that it will just be there. We *become* soul mates. We do not necessarily begin that way.

I have tried to combine the use of practical rules and guidelines for each principle and discuss the studies and explanations that allow understanding of the concepts that underlie them. It is important that a person understand why something is true before behavior can change. Practical suggestions and exercises are included in some chapters to aid you. You may use them repeatedly during your marriage to see how your skills develop or as a reference to work on a specific rule.

This book testifies that marriage can work. Relationships can and should be satisfying. True intimacy and sharing should be part of our lives. We should be soul mates! Do you want to be with someone for eternity with whom you have little in common, no emotional or spiritual intimacy, and little trust? Does that sound like an eternal marriage? No! We must learn to be celestial soul mates. It takes work, and society does not prepare us for that part. It takes effort because it means changing ourselves, evolving, and becoming better people together. We need to develop ourselves so that we can connect spiritually to our spouse and communicate heart to heart and soul to soul.

The Lord said:

> There is a law, irrevocably decreed in heaven before the foundations of this world, upon which all blessings are predicated—And when we obtain any blessing from God, it is by obedience to that law upon which it is predicated. (D&C 130:20–21)

I believe that these are some of the eternal principles on which good relationships are based, and a couple who follows these rules will become more that just spouses—they will become celestial soul mates. Good luck!

Rule 1

Love, Honor, and Cherish

Love is patient. Love is kind. It does not envy, it does not boast, it is not proud. It is not rude, it is not self-seeking, it is not easily angered. It keeps no record of wrongs. Love always protects, always trusts, always hopes, always perseveres. Love never fails.

—See 1 Corinthians 13:4–8

Gardeners know that certain plants grow better when planted together. Whether you have planted mint near the beans or carrots next to the onions, these plants are in symbiosis; they each gain from the other. The mint with its acute perfume keeps insects away from the bean plants, and at the same time, it flourishes better in the shade provided by the taller bean plant. The carrots keep away the parasites of the onions, and the smell of the onion does the same for the carrot parasite. Sometimes plants or flowers planted together just look better, like the Japanese peach blossom and forsythias. They bloom together in early spring, and the dark pink of the Japanese peach blossom is a beautiful contrast to the bright yellow of the forsythias.

These are enduring, intimate relationships. Two plants, each individuals, when planted together, intertwine and become something better, more beautiful than each does by itself. Each draws strength from the other and protects the other. For the plants to grow, certain elements are necessary. There must be good, deep soil. It must contain the proper nutrients for both plants to grow, and there has to be the proper acidity. There must be air and room to grow. One plant cannot suffocate the other. They both need sunshine. Finally, there has to be water, for without water the plants will shrivel and dry up.

In the same way, the marriage of two people needs certain essential elements. There has to be the soil of commitment, the constant supply of the water of respect, and the sunshine of love and affection. Other nutrients need to be added, such as communication and romance, and the soil should never become too acidic.

Each plant must grow and flower, and the Japanese peach blossom should admire the forsythias just as the forsythias takes pleasure in the growth and flowers of the Japanese peach blossom. Neither should try to outdo or suffocate the other. Finally, their roots will grow deeper, and they will become stronger plants with the adversities of life. But they will face them better if they are united. Each year, they will grow, become larger, and be more radiant and joyful. This is the relationship of soul mates. It is the tale of two plants that either grow and fulfill their individual and mutual destinies or that shrivel and would be better off alone. Let us see how a plant grows.

TO LOVE

The traditional marriage ceremony begins with a question asked first to the groom: "Will you . . . take . . . to be your lawfully wedded wife to love, honor, and cherish her?" The same question is then asked to the bride.

Both commit to those three principles: to love, honor, and cherish. The temple ceremony uses different words, but the concept is the same. We need to love, honor, and cherish our spouse. Like many things that we repeat often, these principles become routine and lose significance. You may wonder how people who have gone through this ceremony have thought about what it means to love, honor, and cherish their spouse.

When we ask thirty people to define love, it is not uncommon to find thirty different answers. Poets, writers, and songwriters each have added their own perspectives. Take a minute now and write down your definition of love. Write it down and keep it for a comparison as you continue reading. Do it now!

LOVE IS . . .

If you are like the vast majority of people, somewhere in your definition, you probably have written words like *emotion, feeling,* or *state.* Even though we find many different variations on the word *love,* most people agree that it is some sort of feeling.

I suggest that this is not true. I suggest that love is far more than just an emotion or feeling, and I believe that Satan has purposefully led us astray with this idea. Love as just a feeling has two fallacies. First, it suggests that it is a passive state that we "fall into" or "out of." Second, it suggests that it must be stimulated or initiated by some external event. To understand more fully, let's examine just what an emotion is.

Emotions, contrary to what we normally assume, are automatic and unconscious. They are a reaction to some external stimulus. They are internal physiological and psychological experiences in which the physiological reaction comes first. This is easiest to recognize in the case of fear.

If you are faced with a growling tiger, you will have an automatic physical reaction as soon as the visual stimulus of the tiger arrives to your lower brain. Even before you can analyze it, your body already starts reacting to the situation. It does this by increasing heartbeat, breathing, muscle tension, and adrenaline, among other physiological changes. It increases your aggression and decreases your ability to think and reason. This is because the body diverts blood from the brain to the muscles to increase your power to fight off the threat or run from it.

In psychology, this whole reaction is called the Fright-Flight-Fight Syndrome. Thus, an emotion is both a physiological and psychological event provoked by external stimulus that causes either the arousal of the body, as in fear and anger, or the slowing down of the body, as in boredom or depression. Does this describe love? Is it indeed just a physiological reaction to something that happens to us?

This is an important question because if love isn't just an emotion, what is it? There is another aspect of emotions that should be considered. Because an emotion is a physiological state and not just a psychological state, it is, by necessity, short-lived. Emotions are ephemeral; they come and go, they change and mutate, and they never last very long. Non-arousing emotions tend to last longer than arousing emotions, but even these usually last no more than days at the longest. If love were an emotion, it too would be temporary and transient, here today and gone tomorrow. If love instead lasts years or a lifetime and can evoke just about any emotion from tenderness and contemplation to lust and frustration, then it must be more than a simple emotion.

My bounty is as boundless as the sea, my love as deep; the more I give to thee the more I have, for both are endless.[1]

—William Shakespeare

One way of understanding this is to use the following definitions. When we have an emotion consistently paired with the same thoughts, we have a feeling. When we have a feeling coupled with actions and perceptions, we have an attitude. When attitudes are about complex and abstract issues, we call it a belief.

Love, then, is not just an emotion but describes a whole set of attitudes toward a person that influence perceptions and behaviors. Love is a belief that leads to behaviors that conform to that belief. In fact, the word *love* has origin as a verb: to love. It is an action verb and requires a direct object, as in, "I love someone or something." This means that not only do I have a warm feeling for someone, but also I do something for that person. It is not merely the emotion and not even the accompanying thoughts about the person but implies that some positive action be directed toward that person for his benefit.

Thus, love is not just an emotional state. It is *not* something that comes and goes according to how I am feeling that day, but rather it is a whole collection of thoughts, attitudes, perceptions, and positive emotions about a person that pushes me to act on behalf of that person.

This is an important concept because if we believe that love is just a feeling, then to us it is a passive state—something that happens to us without our will. We often say things like "he has fallen in love," or "she's in love." Thus, we describe some mysterious state that someone falls into. We can just as mysteriously fall out of this state at some future date, and none of this depends on us. We are the passive recipients of this grace. Nothing is required of us. This leads to the other important misconception about love. Because we perceive love as something to feel, this feeling is dependent on someone or something else. All emotions are triggered by some stimulus, and we are the passive recipients of that stimulus. Therefore, if you do something for me, the emotion is triggered, I will feel love, and then I will do something for you. I feel love; therefore I will love. I will love you and therefore will do something for you based on what you do for me. If you do nothing for me, I will not love you. Does this sound like the love of soul mates?

Love is the gentle smile of love upon the lips of beauty.[2]

— Kahil Gibrain

Let's examine an alternative theory about love that results from the psychology of attitude and belief formation. When we investigate complex beliefs that involve thoughts, emotions, and actions, we find that any time there is a contrast between the thoughts and the behavior, it is the behavior that is the most important aspect. We call this cognitive dissonance.

For example, if I love to eat chocolate (behavior) but know that I am overweight and chocolate is bad for me (belief), I have several options. I can change my behavior to conform to my belief, or change the belief to conform to the behavior, or rationalize the importance of the belief—that is, I can stop eating chocolate, change my belief that chocolate leads to weight gain, or rationalize my belief about the dangers of being overweight or how much influence chocolate has. Most often, we rationalize or change our beliefs. Rarely is a belief strong enough to change behavior. The conclusion is that our behaviors govern, for the most part, our beliefs, and not the other way around. What does this have to do with love?

If love, in truth, is a combination of emotions, thoughts, and actions that create a belief about someone or something, then the emotions and thoughts are evoked by the action. It is what *I do* for my spouse in a caring relationship that stimulates the loving feeling in me, not necessarily what my spouse does for me. This is the paradox of love—I do not need to sit and wait for my spouse to do something for me to feel love; rather it is what *I* do that generates the loving feeling within me. Love is proactive. If I want to feel more love, I need to give more to my beloved.

I first encountered this principle on my mission. After only a couple of months in the field, a General Authority visited us and interviewed each missionary. When it was my turn, he asked me about my mission. One of the questions he asked me was how my relationship with my companion was. I replied that it was terrible and launched into a series of criticisms of my companion. He listened and then told me: "If you want to improve your relationship and learn to love your companion so that you can do the work of the Lord, you can do this one action. Get up a half an hour earlier every morning and shine the shoes of your companion."

At the time, I thought he was crazy. I never followed his advice, and I never got along with my companion. His words, however, stuck with me, and it wasn't until I was married that I learned the importance of this concept. If you want to feel love for your eternal companion, don't wait for her to do something for you, but do something for her.

This is easier to understand if we change the context of the situation. If you volunteer to work at a shelter for the homeless, why do you get a good feeling? It is not because the people at the shelter are doing something for you. Isn't it because you are giving service without expecting anything in return? In fact, if they were to pay you to do the same job, you would probably lose that warm, positive feeling. Isn't it the same in a relationship?

If I want to feel love for my mate, I must love her—that is, I must do something for her. It is when I satisfy her needs that I feel the most love. Love is proactive. Love is service.

To feel love, I should not be waiting for my spouse to do something nice for me, but rather I should be doing something positive for her. Love is service. The more I serve, the more I feel love. It is a question of cognitive dissonance. My attitude toward a person will correspond with my actions toward that person. As our mothers told us, it is better to give than to receive. The more I invest in a relationship (behaviors, time, energy), the more my emotions and thoughts will be correspondingly positive. The consequence of this is that if I am not feeling love, I must do something to change that feeling by freely acting in a loving way toward my mate.

The best example of this is our feelings toward our children. Many people, especially mothers, will say that they love their children as much as they love their husband. (Some even say more!) Rationally, this makes little sense. Children require great sacrifice, time, effort, and money, and cause psychological stress, while giving very little back, except an occasional smile or hug. Children are takers, not givers. Think back on the sleepless nights, the vomit on your best clothes, the ruined furniture, and the countless other sacrifices. Where is the reward? Nevertheless, we love them. In fact, we love them dearly. Why? It is because we have given. We have satisfied their needs. We have invested huge amounts of ourselves in them, and we cannot take that back. So, this effort creates cognitive dissonance that influences our emotions, thoughts, and attitudes to correspond with our investment. We love because we have given. Mothers tend to love more because they have invested more. Pregnancy and early childcare are mostly the mother's commitment and investment in the child. She, who has sacrificed the most, loves the most. Only later, as fathers interact more and contribute more to childcare will they start experiencing the same emotions. A father who contributes very little denies himself the opportunity of loving his child.

Another example of this comes from a story told by J. Allen Petterson, a well-known marriage counselor and author. The story can be summarized as follows: A wife seeks help from her pastor stating that she can no longer stand her husband. After many years of marriage, there is no sentiment left. He never tells her that he loves her, and he barely talks to her at all. Their evenings are spent watching TV or reading the newspaper. All her efforts for him are ignored, as are her needs. She feels unloved, angry, and sad, and just cannot put up with it anymore. The children are grown up, and she needs a more fulfilling life. The pastor, instead of expressing sympathy, asks her in a rather sneaky way, "If he has been so mean to you, and so selfish for these many years, wouldn't you really like to get back at him?"

Taken aback by the question but intrigued by the idea, the woman says, "Yes, I would really like to make him suffer as much as he had made me."

The pastor replies, "Good. Here is what you should do. To make him suffer, you first have to make him fall madly in love with you again, as it was at the beginning. Then, just when he is really in love—then you dump him. That way he will really suffer."

The lady thinks for a moment and says, "I like it—I'll do it!"

"Remember," the pastor says, "you will probably have to sacrifice for several months by doing all those things you did in the beginning to make him love you. You will fix his favorite meals and give special attention to his needs. Are you willing to do this?"

The woman replies, "Yes, I'll do it." They make an appointment to meet again after three months to see how the experiment is going and to decide when would be the right moment to dump the husband.

After several months have passed and the pastor still had not heard from this woman, he finally calls her to hear how things are going. The woman answers the phone and upon hearing the pastor's voice, says, "You rat! You knew this was going to happen didn't you?"

Feigning innocence the pastor asks, "What happened?"

The woman says, "It was all going so well. I was fixing his favorite meals. I would no longer nag or needle him to talk to me or to turn off the TV. I started getting up with him in the mornings again and fixing his breakfast—I was doing everything possible to make him fall in love, and it worked. He fell in love again. He started bringing me flowers and gave more attention to my needs. He even turned the TV off some nights to talk."

"So, what is the problem?" the pastor asks.

The lady replies, "Now I have fallen in love with him again! You knew this would happen, didn't you?"[3]

This story also illustrates the point that when you act consistently to serve someone, it touches his soul and he too will open up and serve you, so that love breeds love. There is a counter part to this.

Love is a belief and, like any belief, it is based on trust. We are willing to invest and act unselfishly as long as we believe and we trust that we will be reciprocated at least in part. Mothers can make huge sacrifices and feel totally appeased with just a quick hug every once in a while from their children. The same can be true of couples. If just one spouse invests and gets nothing in return, trust is broken and the feeling dies in the end. It is betrayal that kills love—not just sexual betrayal but betrayal of that basic trust of what a couple considers its relationship to be. This perception, in turn, is based on our expectations. This will be addressed further in Rule 4: Forget the Fantasy.

True love is unconditional. I will continue to serve my loved one and have affectionate thoughts for her unconditionally, as long as there is trust. As long as I believe in my spouse, I will love her.

A basic law of human nature says that when we realize that someone gives unselfishly of himself to us, we will be motivated and stimulated to give back. Therefore, if we desire change in our spouse, it is by changing ourselves that we will achieve it. It is with our loving actions that we will see an increase in the loving actions of our spouse.

Love is proactive. If you want love, *you* must show love. *You* must begin. It is not a passive state in which we wait around for someone to show us love so that we feel the emotion.

There is also a law that says I must have received unconditional love at some time in my life to know how to give. It is the primary duty of parents to love their children, to invest and sacrifice for them so that they can grow up and become loving adults. When this does not happen, the child will have a more difficult time learning to love. He will need much of the unconditional love of his mate to learn how to give.

There is a final aspect of love that must be considered. Love does not mean always having to please the other person, nor does it mean sacrificing our growth for them. Always saying yes to my spouse or my children does not show that I love them. Love is working for the good of the other person. Love means contributing to the spiritual growth of a spouse or a child, and that often requires saying no. It often means confronting the person about his weaknesses but showing our trust and support for him. Too often we hear the phrases "he loved me *in his own way*" or "she loved me *but didn't know how to communicate it.*" If what we do or say inhibits the growth of our mate, it is not love. At the same time, as I work for the spiritual growth of my loved one, that enhances me and I grow too.

The Lord has expressed this concept well in section 121 of the Doctrine and Covenants:

> Reproving betimes with sharpness, when moved upon by the
> Holy Ghost; and then showing forth afterwards an increase of
> love toward him whom thou hast reproved, lest he esteem thee to
> be his enemy; That he may know that thy faithfulness is stronger
> than the cords of death. (D&C 121:43–44)

In his book *The Road Less Traveled*, Dr. Scott Peck defines love as "the total commitment to the full development of the potential of the other."[4]

The measure of love in a relationship is comparable to the spiritual growth of both members of the couple. The more we grow personally, the deeper the relationship becomes. The ultimate goal is to touch souls on a higher plane and become soul mates.

To summarize, love is not an emotion. It is a sum of emotions, thoughts, perceptions, and actions directed toward the spiritual growth of another person. It is not transient but long lasting. To increase our love, we must try to satisfy the needs of the person we love and stimulate her growth. The more we do for that person, the better we feel about him. To love means to get out of bed an hour earlier to have breakfast with your spouse, to clean the house even though you dislike housework, to go out in the evening even if you are tired. It means to do the hundreds of little things every day so that your spouse feels your love. As Stephen Covey says, "To do carefully and constantly and kindly many little things is not a little thing."[5] On the other hand, as the Seneca said thousands of years ago, "If you wish to be loved, love."[6]

One of my favorite poems by Elizabeth Barrett Browning sums up these feelings:

How Do I Love Thee?

How do I love thee? Let me count the ways
I love thee to the depth and breadth and height
My Soul can reach, when feeling out of sight
For the ends of Being and ideal Grace.
I love thee to the level of everyday's
Most quiet need, by sun and candle-light.
I love thee freely, as men strive for Right;
I love thee purely, as they turn from Praise.
I love thee with the passion put to use
In my old griefs, and with my childhood faith.
I love thee with a love I seemed to lose
With my lost Saints—I love thee with the breath

Smiles, tears, of all my life!—and, if God choose,
I shall but love thee better after death.[7]

TO HONOR AND TO CHERISH

The media, Hollywood, and people in general constantly debate, discuss, and analyze love. The meaning of "to honor and to cherish" is ignored. Honor is defined as "a person of superior standing," or, "one whose worth brings respect," or finally, "an evidence of distinction."[8] The synonyms used are homage, reverence, and deference. In Hebrew, to honor means "to bend one's knee, to revere." Another definition is "to hold in awe, or to hold in high value."

To honor is not just to respect your spouse, a necessary first step, but also to hold him in high esteem.

Walking into the room where your spouse is should be like walking into a room where someone you admire is sitting. If you were to enter a restaurant and the prophet or an apostle were there, or if Bill Gates, Oprah Winfrey, or Magic Johnson were in the room, what would your reaction be? Wouldn't it probably be something like, "Wow!" You would probably feel grateful that you are in the same room with someone so famous or admirable. You might watch him constantly, maybe discreetly out of the corner of your eye, and you would pay him considerable attention. This does not mean that you have low self-esteem or that you believe that this person is much better than you are but that you respect and admire this person. You should feel the same way when you are with your spouse—this is what it means to honor him or her. Do you say to yourself, "Wow!" when your wife walks into the room? Are you ever in awe of your husband's abilities?

To cherish is very similar. Cherish is defined as "to hold dear, to treat with care and affection, to keep deeply in mind."[9] To hold dear means to hold your mate as someone extremely valuable and worthy of being honored and admired. Think of the most valuable material possession you own. Where do you keep it? How do you treat it? What are your feelings about it? If we have a valuable piece of jewelry, we usually do not leave it lying on the couch or thrown on the kitchen table. We keep it in a jewelry box, maybe on a velvet cushion, and if it is valuable enough, locked in a safe. We take care of it. We spend time and energy assuring ourselves that it is safe. We cherish it.

In terms of relationships, there are two fundamental questions:

1. Is your spouse the most important person in your life?
2. Does he know that?

To honor and cherish your spouse means to make that person your number one priority and to communicate that through words and behavior so that he is convinced of it.

If we are capable of this, we probably do not need any of the other rules of relationships. Too often, a spouse's complaint of the other spouse is that he has made someone else or something else more important than their relationship. He does not show honor anymore. Stop and contemplate again those two questions. Are you sure that you have made your eternal mate the most important thing in your life? In your priorities, is your spouse number one? Would you sacrifice everything else to keep your spouse and make her happy? Does your spouse know this? How have you shown it?

When you make your career more important than your mate, you will lose her. When you make your child more important than your spouse, you will lose him. Above all, when your own selfish desires are more important than your relationship with your spouse, you will lose him. Even making religion more important than your spouse is not the answer because one of the ways we show our love for God is by loving the person whom we have vowed to serve and honor.

It is true that there are times when we have to dedicate much time and energy to build our careers, to nurture our children, or to perform our church duties. Sometimes this means not being there for our mate. This, however, will make little difference in the relationship if our spouse understands that we are doing it for the benefit of the relationship itself, and that she is still our number one priority. Let me repeat what I said.

To honor and cherish your spouse means to make that person your number one priority and to communicate that through words and behavior so that she is convinced of it.

One of our basic human needs is to be validated. To be validated means that someone recognizes us as a unique human being and that they consider us special. Think back to when you and your spouse first met and fell in love. Why did you feel loved? Wasn't it because he made you feel special? Somehow, as you got to know each other profoundly and touched spirits, your spouse made you feel extraordinary and unique. She laughed at your jokes, was moved by the way you smiled, and could not keep away from you. You shared thoughts and emotions. She cherished you; you felt appreciated for just being you. She revered you, was interested in everything you said, and made you feel important. It was that "wow" experience every time you were together.

Keep thinking of that period. What were the things that you did or said that communicated to her your love? What did you do to make him feel special and needed? Are you still doing these things? What are the things that you could start doing today that would make your loved one feel more appreciated?

What are the traits in your mate that attracted you to him? Why was he so special that you preferred him over all others? Why did you decide to marry him? How is he unique? Take a few minutes and write down these traits in your spouse.

I fell madly in love with my spouse because:

1.

2.

3.

4.

5.

When was the last time that you told your husband or wife why you appreciate him or her so much? Why? Let your spouse know today what you appreciate.

One of the most essential human needs is feeling appreciated and needed. These are fundamental ingredients of love. The soil that allows the plants to grow and expand their roots will become barren if we do not communicate to our spouses that we need and appreciate them.

This is much harder to do when you are working ten- or twelve-hour days to create a career or when there are screaming babies, kids fighting, and all the daily chores to do. However, when we no longer communicate at a deep level to our spouses that they are the most important person in our lives, the relationship no longer receives the necessary nutrients it needs to survive.

President Gordon B. Hinckley captured this concept when he said:

> It would be a beautiful world if every girl had the privilege of marriage to a good man whom she could look upon with pride

and gladness as her companion in time and eternity, hers alone to love and cherish, respect, and help. What a wonderful world it would be if every young man were married to a wife in the house of the Lord, one at whose side he would stand as protector, provider, husband, and companion.[10]

Whether your relationship is strong and healthy or has become stale and routine, this is the most important step you can take. Take time today to tell your spouse why he is special to you. Explain why you appreciate him. Write down the unique characteristics of your spouse and why he is special, and put it in a special folder and give it to him. Keep a copy for yourself.

Now that you have communicated this with words, communicate with actions. Do something special for your spouse, something that you know she will appreciate—maybe something that you have not done for a long time. Do it today; do something else tomorrow. Make it a daily behavior.

Love is not just a feeling. It has to be proactive. We have to show it, feed it, and communicate it for it to grow. We have to nurture our relationship; we have to honor our spouses by making them feel precious and appreciated. We need to cherish them.

Here are just a few suggestions of what to do and what not to do to show honor to your spouse and express your love. Add to this list and keep it where you can see it regularly.

1.   Never take your spouse for granted. Husbands, pay attention to your wives. Be observant of what she wears, her appearance, and changes in her hairstyle. Compliment her. Wives, show appreciation for the work your husband does and for how he contributes to the family. Use good manners. Saying please and thank you is not just social etiquette but a form of respect. Take care of yourselves. It's good to be comfortable at home, but wearing dirty, baggy sweats every day may communicate to your spouse that you don't care about his feelings anymore.

2.   Wives, ask your husband for advice or his opinion on issues. Husbands, do the same. One of the greatest needs of a male is to feel competent. Too often, he feels competent and admired at work and degraded and neglected at home. It is not by chance that so many men have affairs with their secretaries. She sees him at work and admires and values him, whereas at home he finds just the opposite. Similarly, many husbands treat their wives as though they were brainless. They criticize their lack of logic—or worse, ignore their opinions.

3.   Praise and compliment your spouse when you are with others. Showing your appreciation in public also shows your commitment and love. Never belittle or criticize your spouse in front of others, not even when joking. There is no better way to demoralize and demean your spouse than to tell stories or episodes that embarrass or slight her.

4.   Do not nag. Nagging is a tactic many wives use to exert pressure on their husband to do something. Rather than feeling motivated to fulfill his responsibilities, he will ignore them. Nagging is another way of making him feel incompetent and irresponsible. Find other ways to motivate him. Nagging is the opposite of trust.

5.   Discover and appreciate your spouse's occupation. Can you accurately describe what your spouse does all day and what his responsibilities are? Do you appreciate the skills and talents that your spouse displays on the job? This is particularly true for husbands whose wives are homemakers and mothers. There is no job that compares to the need for creativity, time management, organizational skills, and just plain stamina than that of being a mother. Husbands, try taking the responsibilities of the house and the children for a week, and you will end up with great admiration for your wife.

6.   Find out what other people admire in your mate. Too often we take certain characteristics for granted. Ask your mutual friends and your spouse's co-workers what they admire in your spouse.

7.   Compliment often. To hold admiration in your heart is not sufficient; you must communicate it in a meaningful way. Do not make a generic compliment. Saying, "You look good," is not very effective, particularly if you always say the same thing. In fact, it is almost disqualifying. It is far better to say, "I really like the way that sweater matches your skirt; you have good taste in color matching," or "That color really brings out the blue in your eyes and makes you even more handsome." Women are far better at this than men are, but men can and need to learn how to give more meaningful compliments.

Continue this list on your own.

To love, to honor, and to cherish your spouse is the fundamental rule of a satisfying and fulfilling relationship. All the other rules in this book are corollaries to this. This type of unconditional love and admiration is not necessarily what we begin with in a relationship. In the beginning, we have the positive disposition to love, but then the relationship evolves, and it takes hard work to achieve and maintain a friendship and companionship that will grow and prosper. It is sometimes difficult to overcome the urge to change our spouse into someone we want him to be. But we need to love and appreciate his uniqueness.

In their book *Becoming Soul Mates*, Les and Leslie Parrot explain that most trees have root systems that grow as deep as the leaf line of the tree is wide and high. This is not true, however, of the mighty redwood that has a very shallow root system that spreads out in all directions but remains on the surface. A redwood standing alone can easily be blown over because the lack of deep roots makes it vulnerable. When two redwoods grow together, however, their root systems intertwine, and they gain strength from each other to withstand the winds and fury of the elements. It is almost impossible to blow them over.[11] So is life as soul mates; our roots intertwine, and though we may each be weak alone, we become strong together. We support and sustain each other against the furies of the world and stand strong together.

The Lord said the same in Ecclesiastes 4:9–12:

> Two are better than one; because they have good reward for their labor. For if they fall, the one will lift up his fellow: but woe to him that is alone when he falleth; for he hath not another to help him up. Again, if two lie together they have heat, but how can one be warm alone? And if one prevail against him, two shall withstand him, and a threefold cord is not quickly broken.

NOTES
1. Ben Whitley, *Words of Love* (Kansas City: Hallmark Cards, Inc., 1970).
2. Ibid.
3. Allan J. Petterson. Cassette tapes. "How to Stay in Love," *A Winning Marriage* (Wheaton, IL: Family Concern).
4. M. Scott Peck, *The Road Less Traveled* (New York: Simon & Schuster), 1978.
5. Stephen R. Covey, *The 7 Habits of Highly Effective Families* (New York: Golden Books, 1997), 51.
6. Lucius Annaeus Seneca. Online. *Brainy Quote*; available from www.brainyquote.com.
7. Elizabeth Barrett Browning. Online. "XLIII How Do I Love Thee," *Sonnets from the Portuguese;* available from www.amherst.edu.
8. Merriam-Webster Dictionary (New York: Simon & Schuster), 1974.
9. Ibid.
10. Gordon B. Hinckley, *Teachings of Gordon B. Hinckley* (LDS Library 2006), 601.
11. Les and Leslie Parrott, *Becoming Soul Mates* (Grand Rapids: Zondervan, 1995), 209.

Rule 2

COMMIT FOR THE BAD TIMES

If thou faint in the day of adversity, thy strength is small.
—Proverbs 24:10

In informal surveys of many hundreds of students in my classes, I ask which elements are necessary for a successful marriage. The most popular response is trust.

Some people have more difficulty trusting than others. This is often caused by our own childhoods and the love we received or did not receive. Trust in others begins with the trust our parents created in us by taking care of our needs. When this basic trust in others is lacking, it will be more difficult to create trust in the relationship. Therapy may help, or the distrusting person may need a spouse who can give even more trust, love, and commitment. The process, however, is true for all people—we need time to ascertain the commitment of the other person to us. We open up a little at a time and unveil our feelings and innermost emotions and thoughts one layer at a time according to how we are accepted and according to how much the other person reciprocates the process.

The human heart, at whatever age, opens only to the heart that opens in return.
—Mary Edgeworth[1]

Edgeworth's quote is the reason that dating and courtship are part of most modern societies—so we can find out the level of trust and acceptance by testing out different possible spouses *before* we commit to each other. Once we have built the trust and have committed ourselves to each other, we have to know that the commitment is for the good times and bad times, in sickness and in health. If we don't believe in our spouses, the love and the relationship cannot continue to grow.

Trust is the fundamental element of becoming soul mates. How can we touch someone's soul? Even more important, how can we let them touch ours if we do not have complete trust in that person?

In his book *Bridges*, Richard Bach describes the role of a soul mate:

> A soul mate is someone who has locks that fit our keys, and keys to fit our locks. When we feel safe enough to open the locks, our truest selves step out and we can be completely and honestly who we are; we can be loved for who we are and not for who we are pretending to be. Each unveils the best part of the other. No matter what else goes wrong around us, with that one person we're safe in our own paradise. Our soul mate is someone who shares our deepest longings, our sense of direction. When we are two balloons, and together our direction is up, chances are we've found the right person. Our soul mate is the one who makes life come to life.[2]

Trust is based on two important principles: honesty and commitment.

HONESTY

When talking about relationships in my classes, the subject that elicits the most heated debate is the need for honesty. Many people opt for dishonesty, or fudging the truth. The dictionary defines honesty as "free from deception, truthful, genuine and real, or marked by integrity."[3] How can two people enter into a loving, lasting relationship with deception? How can two souls touch spirits if one is not truthful with the other? How can you have absolute trust if there is deception and lying? How can we be genuine and real with each other if we are not honest?

How can I feel true love if I know that I have held back parts of myself—usually the most negatives parts? There will always remain in my mind the doubt that if she *really* knew me intimately, my spouse might not like me at all. Another word closely linked to honesty is sincerity. This has an interesting root as it comes from the Latin *sinc cera,* or "without wax." Seemingly, it was a common practice among the Romans when building the palaces for the wealthy of the city to fudge on the budget. Marble, even then, was expensive and hard to obtain, so rather than construct the pillars of the palace with solid marble, the inner part was made of wax and then covered with a marble facade. The pillars kept the external beauty, but obviously, the wax columns were more likely to collapse.

Is it any different in a relationship? If we put up a facade with our mate, we may look good, but the relationship is weak and may eventually collapse. We have to be genuine and sincere with our spouse. Anything less mars our soul, and we lose that intimate communication.

We are trained to distrust from a young age when we find people who take advantage of our vulnerabilities in order to hurt us. Think back to the taunts of your schoolmates or your older brothers or sisters and the hurt you felt. To avoid the taunts, the criticisms, and the emotional pain, we close up and create fronts. This is why it takes time to establish the absolute trust necessary to unfold and share our innermost feelings and experiences. When we find ourselves holding back, it means we either have not reached that degree of trust or we had it but something has disturbed it, causing us to be afraid of getting hurt. If you find yourself not opening up to your spouse, this is the moment to analyze what has happened to your relationship.

An honest answer is like a kiss on the lips.

—Proverbs 24:26

Honesty and sincerity begin with ourselves. We must be honest with our own feelings. Rather than suppressing our feelings, we should be honest enough to acknowledge and accept them and discover why we feel that way. If I am angry with my spouse but suppress that anger or divert it to the children or someone else, what have I accomplished? I should accept that I am angry and try to understand why. What has my spouse done that has hurt me or threatened me? Why have I experienced this reaction? Were my perceptions and expectations realistic? How did I contribute to the situation? We must be honest about our own limitations and not try to excuse ourselves by blaming our spouse. We must become genuine, real people who can share ourselves openly with our soul mates.

With honesty, people tend to go to one extreme or the other. Either they hide parts of themselves and are unable to be sincere, or they believe that sincerity means saying everything on their mind, no matter how offensive it may be. Neither is correct. The first example limits intimacy and will hinder the special relationship of friendship and touching of your spirits. The opposite can be more destructive. Insults, sarcasm, demeaning remarks, criticizing with intent to harm, and extreme anger are no way to honor, cherish, or express love to your spouse. They are merely a lack of self-control and a sign of immaturity. "Letting it all out" is not honesty but childlike behavior, like the temper tantrums of a three-year-old. All feelings, including anger, can be communicated in appropriate ways and at the right time. Once I have discovered within myself why I feel the anger and realize how I participated in the process, I can then communicate this to my spouse to solve the problem. The Lord has said, "Speaking the truth in love. . . . Let no corrupt communication proceed out of your mouth, but that which is good to the use of edifying, that it may administer grace unto the hearers" (Ephesians 4:15, 29).

Another excuse for being dishonest is that we do not want to hurt our spouse's feelings. It is true that sometimes our wives ask us, "How do I look?" or "Do you like this dress?" Being honest need not be brutal. There are diplomatic ways of letting her know that you preferred her old hairdo or a different dress. One student offered this advice: "Always be perfectly honest about your preference before she buys the dress, but keep quiet once the dress is bought!" If we have at heart the best for our spouse, honesty never interferes. When a man says that he has not told his spouse about an affair because he does not want to hurt her feelings, he is not respecting or worrying about his wife's feelings. If that were true, he would never have had the affair. Rather, he is afraid of her reaction and thus protects himself.

Reckless words pierce like a sword, but the tongue of the wise brings healing.
—Proverbs 12:18

Are you honest with yourself? Do you admit your errors, or are you always blaming others? Are you a complainer? Being honest with yourself is not easy; it requires taking responsibility for your actions, thoughts, emotions, and reactions.

Can you talk about any subject with your spouse? Are there subjects that you avoid mentioning? Why? Take a moment to think about these issues. Many issues may be the lingering pain caused by an unresolved conflict. By not resolving your conflicts, you have erected barriers that will limit spiritual intimacy with your spouse. Other avoided subjects may be secrets from your past or present. All secrets create walls and breed dishonesty. They will eventually strangle your relationship. Why don't you trust your mate enough to share these parts of your life?

Are you genuine and sincere with your mate? Can you talk from your heart about any subject with him or her? Can you share your emotions? Do you feel that he or she accepts you the way you are? Do you accept your mate? One good test of trust is whether you can open up totally in your prayers to the Lord in the presence of your spouse. Is there a big difference between your individual prayers and your shared prayers? Why?

Criticism and disapproval are two elements that ruin honesty and trust. If I open up to my spouse and she openly judges me and makes slighting remarks about what I have just said, it will be a long time before I will open my heart to her again. I cannot control my mate's reactions, but I can work on mine. Often, it is my constant criticism or disapproval that impedes my mate from being sincere. If, whenever my spouse states her thoughts or feelings I belittle her or act condescendingly, she will learn not to express herself anymore.

James had much to say in his epistle about those who cannot bridle their tongue:

> And the tongue is a fire, a world of iniquity: so is the tongue among our members, that it defileth the whole body, and setteth on fire the course of nature; and it is set on fire of hell. . . . Out of the same mouth proceedeth blessing and cursing. My brethren, these things ought not to be so. (James 3: 6, 10)

We build honesty with acceptance and appreciation. Only when I accept my mate for who she is, without judgment or criticism, will she show me a deeper and more meaningful glimpse of her inner soul. As I accept and appreciate and open up my heart, she can unfold more layers of herself until we are totally exposed and in touch with each other. This is why constantly trying to change your mate, to mold him or her into someone else, is so damaging. In essence, you are saying, "I don't like you or accept you the way you are." If I want my mate to open up more, I must accept her for who she is today. I must appreciate her uniqueness and not try to change her or mold her into someone else. This destroys honesty and trust.

Thus, honesty and sincerity lead to trust, which increases and allows us to further expose ourselves and be more open and genuine, which further augments trust. This cycle will continue until we have totally opened up to our spouse, we have no secrets, and we can read each other's heart and soul. No facades, no barriers, no clouded, obscure areas inhibit our sincere communication. This may seem too idealistic, but we should strive for this goal. This is what it means to be soul mates.

Commitment

On a perfect day, I know that I can count on you
When that's not possible, tell me can you weather the storm
'Cause I need somebody who will stand by me

Through the good times and bad times
She will always, always be right there
Sunny days, everybody loves them
Tell me can you stand the rain
Storms will come, this we know for sure
Can you stand the rain?[4]

—Boyz II Men

It is not enough to be honest. This trust and sincerity must stand the test of time and tribulations.

The traditional marriage formula uses the phrase "to love, honor, and cherish *in good times and bad times, in sickness and health.*" This phrase seems to have lost significance in our society. Many leave it out of the marriage ceremony or ignore it, but this is the most essential phrase of all. If love is based on trust, then trust is based on this commitment, *in good times and bad times, in sickness and health.*

There was a phrase coined during the American Revolution used with great disdain—"a fair weather friend." A fair weather friend was a farmer who would come and give a hand to the revolutionaries only when his crops were planted and chores done and if there was good weather. When winter arrived or the times got rough, more than half of Washington's army would disappear to go back home. A fair weather friend was someone who could not commit to a cause but wanted to seem friendly. It seems that many married people today are just "fair weather friends." When difficulties arise, they are ready to run away.

John, in Revelation said it another way: "I know thy works, that thou art neither cold nor hot: I would thou wert cold or hot. So then because thou art lukewarm, and neither cold nor hot, I will spue thee out of my mouth" (Rev. 3–15,16). People who cannot commit have been considered worse than the enemy because they have no cause, no strong belief. Do we see this in marriage?

On the other hand, during pioneer days in the west, another phrase referred to a good companion, whether male or female: "someone to ride the river with." This affirmation was apparently created during the trail drives from Texas. Many of the tasks of the cowboy or pioneer were arduous and dangerous, but one of the most difficult and life threatening was crossing the rivers with the herds. It was necessary for the cowboys to string out the cows downstream and behind them and literally drive them across. Many longhorns would try to bolt, and the cowboys in the river were most at risk, both from the currents and from being speared or trampled from the longhorns. Thus, "someone to ride the river with" refers to someone with the courage to stick through the difficult and dangerous times. Which would you prefer—a "fair weather friend" or "someone to ride the river with?"

Which are you? Couples who plan on marrying should critically examine this issue. Is my girlfriend or boyfriend committed? How does my prospective spouse show this? Could I trust him with my life? How has she demonstrated that she is worthy of this trust? Will he stick through thick and thin, or is he a fair weather friend?

It is interesting to note that trees, shrubs, and large plants that are planted in the spring rarely thrive. In the abundant rains of spring, they do not develop deep roots that will sustain them during the dry summer months or the freezing weather of winter. It is better to plant the trees in the fall so that the roots will grow deep, deeper than the frozen surface to absorb the nutrients from even the driest soil. So too are relationships. Relationships that flourish in the sun and abundant rains without difficulties may not develop the strong roots necessary for the relationship to endure. We should be thankful for life's adversities that allow us to demonstrate our love and devotion to each other. This will create the roots that will keep the plant strong and vigorous throughout life.

> *"Nothing, so it seems to me," said the stranger, "is more beautiful than the love that has weathered the storms of life."*[5]
> —Jerome K. Jerome, *Three Men in a Boat*

To invest ourselves, our love, our energy, and our money in a relationship, we have to believe that it is going to last. Otherwise, there will always be the tendency to hold back and say, "Let's wait and see."

One of the great paradoxes of our time is the failure of cohabitation as a prelude to a happy marriage. The idea was proposed many years ago but gained acceptance in the sexual freedom of the sixties because the concept was so logical. Divorces in the sixties became frequent, and the reason given most often was incompatibility of character. Therefore, it made sense to say, "Let's live together for a while (months or years) and see how we do, and if we find that we enjoy it, can get along, and have no sexual incompatibilities, then we can marry."

Because it sounds so reasonable, many couples today cohabit before they marry, and faithful members of the Church may feel that they are missing something when they don't follow the example of so many of their peers. Astonishingly, the statistics all indicate that marriages formed after cohabitation are shorter than marriages in which the couples did not live together. Why? On the surface, it makes no sense.

There are three reasons. One has to do with goals and objectives. Another deals with the change of expectations that will be discussed in the following chapters. The final reason has everything to do with commitment. When I suggest to a spouse, "Let's live together and see how things work out," I am often suggesting one of two things or both. First, I may be saying, "I'm not sure about my ability to commit to you, and I want to try it out first." Alternatively, I am saying, "I'm not sure about you, and I want to try *you* out for a while." Putting a person on trial is a form of conditional love. It is saying that I will make no investment until I am sure that you are responsible, good in bed, and able to satisfy my needs. What should now be a committed relationship is actually a trial with conditional love. Relationships based on conditional love are frequently doomed unless they can transform to unconditional love.

Cohabitation has taken the place of dating and courtship and does not allow the same advantages. When you begin dating, you can open up a little at a time, and you have the option of withdrawing temporarily when you are too vulnerable. You can set the pace of the process of sharing your thoughts and feelings and understanding the other person; therefore, you can be more honest. When two people start living together at the beginning of a relationship, before they have created that deeper sharing experience, they are more likely to erect barriers and facades that will remain with them during their time together. Through cohabitation, you get to know your partner less, not more—or rather you know only the outer fronts and not the true soul of your mate. Even after a couple has cohabited for years and finally decides to commit to marriage, the relationship changes drastically because each spouse finds that the person they thought they knew so well changed.

Too often in relationships, partners imply that they will commit to you as you are right now, but if you change, they are no longer bound to you. Does this sound like someone to ride the river with? The same is true of marriages with a contract. We are specifically stating conditions to our commitment. I will stay with you only if you never gain more than ten pounds. I will be your spouse only if you never raise your voice. This implies that I am bound only if everything goes well. It also says that I love you only because you are thin or quiet. I love just one of your qualities, not you. I do not accept you fully. I am not truly committed to you at all.

The media and society have led us to believe that true love and marriage are set in stone. We fall in love with a wonderful person, and they with us, and we will stay that way forever. The fallacy is to believe that nothing will change; we will remain the same, and our spouse will also stay the same. Again, the media has persuaded us that relationships are between young, beautiful, and healthy people. When the relationship begins, we usually fit that mold, but no one stays that way. There is health, but there is also sickness. If your wife has breast cancer, do you leave her? If your husband loses his job, does this mean the relationship is over? If he is impotent, is he worthless? Not only do we age, gain weight, and get sick, but we also change. The man or woman whom you marry today will not be the same person in five years or ten years from now. This change is not just physical. Ideas and attitudes change as we mature; even our personalities change. Even if I have lived with someone for five years, nothing guarantees that five years from now he or she will be the same. So how do I know that we will be compatible next year, or five years from now? Whether it is cohabitation or marriage, we change and our spouse changes.

We do not commit only to that person as he or she is right now, but we commit to continue to love that special person as he or she changes and evolves. We commit to change and evolve and grow ourselves so that we are better people five years or ten years from now. We commit to continue communicating with love and honesty the changes that occur in us.

Part of the beauty of a relationship is that we have participated in the change and maturation of our mate. As soul mates, we decide to grow and to change and to accept the growth and change of our mate. We begin the relationship with a young and fragile plant, but we expect it to grow to its stature, and we know that we are an essential element in that growth. This, however, takes time, patience, and commitment to the relationship.

We have to work to keep in touch with each other's ideas and changes. We need to exert effort to stay compatible. Part of commitment is saying that I will be of aware of and accept your changes. I will help your spirit grow. I will appreciate your new perceptions and ideas, and I will share mine with you so that we can grow together. The illusion that society gives us is that compatibility is like love—it is either there or it disappears. Nothing is required of us.

Commitment has to be mutual and reciprocal. It requires the humility to admit that not only will our spouse change but we will too. There will be times when it will be difficult to put up with certain behaviors of your husband, but remember that he will have to endure your idiosyncrasies too. There will be times when you are nervous or nagging. Commitment is part of the investment we make to our relationships. It grows by degrees as trust builds.

Many studies have indicated that commitment can be renewed and increased. Six major factors increase commitment. This is not just commitment in a relationship but to any cause, idea, or action. Following these criteria can increase how committed I am to a diet, to a political idea, or to my wife.

1. *The explicitness of the behavior.* How openly I show or communicate my commitment. For example, when I express my commitment to many people publicly.
2. *The importance of the behavior.* When I act in a way that shows how important my commitment is to me.
3. *The degree of irrevocability.* When there are social, legal, or economic consequences because of my commitment.
4. *Number of actions.* The frequency with which I express or repeat behaviors that demonstrate strong commitment.
5. *Degree of volition.* How willingly I display my commitment to others without being forced or persuaded to do so.
6. *Effort.* The more effort and sacrifice the commitment requires the stronger it is.[6]

How explicit the behavior is means that expressing an opinion publicly and openly shows a stronger commitment than expressing the same privately. One of the reasons of the success of programs like Weight Watchers or AA is that they require a public statement of commitment. Weight Watchers has many statistics to confirm that those who come regularly to the meetings and publicly weigh themselves lose weight, and those who do not do so stay the same weight. The difference is not the principles of the program but rather the commitment of the person. The same is true in a relationship. The importance of the behavior refers to whom we express our commitment. Obviously, expressing our resolution to a stranger is less binding than expressing it to our boss. When we tell the world, including our parents, our friends, and our family members of our love, we show far more commitment than if we express it just to our spouse.

In the same way, when there are social and legal consequences to our actions, they become more binding than just words. When two people form a business relationship, they draw up legal papers, invest money, and declare to society that they are a legal entity. This also explains why a legal marriage is always more of a commitment than cohabitation. Marriage implies an important, irrevocable, explicit behavior. We make a statement of our love publicly, in an important way that is legally binding. It is even more important when we also make the commitment to God. This is why society places so much importance on marriage. It is a larger investment, a bigger effort, and it demonstrates our commitment to one another and to this institution. Cohabitation or even elopement seem much easier because they are. When we invite our friends and our relatives to our marriage, we are expressing our love more publicly and more explicitly. We are making a stronger commitment. The fact that this is done according to laws of the land and changes our legal status makes it even more binding. To ignore this because "all we need is our love" is to miss an essential investment for the relationship. You miss the occasion to strongly state your commitment to each other. The largest investment you can make is to make a vow before God, the Church, and all your friends and relatives to enter into an eternal covenant by the power of the holy priesthood.

This, however, is just the beginning. Having a temple wedding but not continuing to express commitment to each other through day-to-day actions and loving words has little relevance to how long the relationship endures. Commitment is an everyday affair. There can be special occasions that allow us to openly express and renew that commitment. Think of the words of Ruth and her expression of commitment:

> And Ruth said, Intreat me not to leave thee, or to return from following after thee: for whither thou goest, I will go; and where thou lodgest, I will lodge: thy people shall be my people, and thy God my God; Where thou diest, will I die and there I will be buried: the Lord do so to me, and more also. (Ruth 1:16–17)

There is a general commitment to be there for each other, to continue to work, and to grow together through the good times and the bad times. But as a couple you can make more specific commitments to each other. Many couples write their own marriage vows, and this is a good time to envision and to publicly express certain commitments that are important to you. This is not the same as a marriage contract in which we put limits on our love, but just the opposite. We commit ourselves to improving the relationship in specific ways. By way of example, Dr. Kevin Leman, in his book *Sex Begins in the Kitchen,* lists ten commitments that he believes are important for couples to make:

1. We commit ourselves to make love a daily choice, even when life looks easier somewhere else.
2. We commit ourselves to treasure each other as gifts from God.
3. We commit ourselves to be quick to forgive and not to hold grudges.
4. We commit ourselves to make time for each other.
5. We commit ourselves to talk daily about our thoughts and feelings.
6. We commit ourselves to show respect for each other, both publicly and privately, avoiding put-downs, selfish demands, and belittling words.
7. We commit ourselves to try to get behind each other's eyes, to understand the other's specific needs.
8. We commit ourselves to do all we can to make sure our marriage has a positive impact on those around us.
9. We commit ourselves to pray for each other and support each other's spiritual growth.
10. We commit ourselves to honor God and each other through our thoughts, words, and actions.[7]

These commitments are specific and go beyond just "not having an affair or cheating on my spouse." Each couple should have specific commitments that they have stated and shared. What are yours? Have you and your spouse ever written your own commitments to each other? If not, get together with your spouse tonight and try it.

We commit ourselves to . . .

1.

2.

3.

4.

5.

Can you come up with ten commandments for your relationship?

Many a man claims to have unfailing love, but a faithful man who can find?
—See Proverbs 20:6

Commitment does not end at marriage. Expressing your love freely and frequently renews the commitment. Doing things for each other on a daily basis does the same. Too often men in particular forget this or are not aware of it. It is not enough to just wash her car for her. It is necessary to express your love both verbally and non-verbally, and to do it often. In addition, your wife should not have to prompt you. The classical exchange between husband and wife is, she says, "I love you," and he replies "Me too," or "Ditto." This is better than nothing, but not much. Husbands, you should remember to tell you wife often, "I love you," or "I cherish you." Write a love note and leave it in her purse, send a text message, or do something special for her on a regular basis. Be creative, and do not let it become just a routine. Flowers every Friday are nice, but soon they lose their importance.

Finally, the love and commitment we express most loudly is in our everyday actions, particularly those that require effort. When we see our mate do something for us that we know requires great effort and sacrifice, we feel most loved. They have shown us their commitment to us. Commitment is the nutrient in the soil of trust that allows the plant to grow. It must be there or the roots of the plant dry out and the plant dies. The seed and newborn plant require a great deal of the sunshine of love and the water of communication. At the very beginning of a relationship when we first plant the seed, we will need constant reassurance of the love of our spouse, or the seed will dry out and we will move on. Equally important, however, is that the seed is planted in fertile soil and that the nutrients of growth be constantly present to allow the growth of the plant. No matter how much of the water of love is poured into sandy, infertile soil, the plant cannot survive. The nutrients have to be replenished during the course of the relationship as the plant grows, or it will not survive.

Commitment and trust are another reason that a relationship becomes stronger over the course of the years than it is in the beginning. The relationship is like a vase of clay. The soft clay can be molded and shaped. This is important in the beginning, but if left as clay, it will eventually collapse and become formless. To make the finished product strong and beautiful, you have to put it in the kiln repeatedly. It is the fire of the kiln that makes the vase strong. The hotter the fire, the stronger and more resistant the ceramic. In the same way, the trials of life make the relationship stronger. No matter how well molded we are, if our relationships have not withstood the fires of life, they will become lifeless. It is the misfortune, the sickness, and the difficult times that allow us to show our commitment to our loved one, and thus increase the trust, love, and investment in our relationship. We know our spouses will be there for us because they have been in the past, and they have the same assurance. Thus we become the perfect vase.

NOTES

1. Story Circle Network. Online; available from storycircle.org.
2. Richard David Bach, *Bridges*. Taken from CD *Quotationary* (NovaSoft, 1999).
3. Merriam-Webster Dictionary (New York: Simon & Schuster, 1974).
4. Boyz II Men, "Can You Stand the Rain," *Evolution* (Motown Record Company, 1999).
5. Jerome K. Jerome, *Three Men in a Boat: to Say Nothing of the Dog* (Ware Hertfordshire, UK: Wordsworth Editions LTD, 1992).
6. Kiesler 1971, as cited in Brehm, Miller, Perlman, and Cambell, *Intimate Relationships* (New York, New York: McGraw-Hill, Inc., 1992), 171.
7. Kevin Leman, *Sex Begins in the Kitchen* (Grand Rapids, Michigan: Fleming H. Revell, 1999), 245-246.

Rule 3

We, Not Me

Thou shalt love thy wife with all thy heart, and shalt cleave unto her and none else.

—Doctrine and Covenants 42:22

For this cause shall a man leave father and mother, and shalt cleave to his wife: and they twain shall be one flesh? Wherefore they are no more twain, but one flesh.

—Matthew 19:5–6

Part of commitment is knowing just what you are pledging. What type of relationship do you intend to create? Please note that the emphasis is on the last five words *do you intend to create.* Like many other myths that we will talk about, most people believe that a relationship just happens. It is a magical quality that is beyond our control. Some people are lucky and have good relationships; others are not and their relationships always go sour. Rarely do we place ourselves as active participants in creating good relationships. Just like love, we think relationships happen or they do not. Instead, just as true love is proactive and depends on what we do, so does our relationship.

The untended garden quickly goes to weeds. My wife is occasionally irritated when friends come by and exclaim, "What a lovely garden you have!" It sounds at times that they think that beautiful gardens just happen. Their gardens would probably be just as splendid if they spent the long hours of tilling, weeding, transplanting, and seeding that my wife does. The same is true for the garden of relationships. A beautiful garden, a beautiful vase, or any work of art first begins in the artist's mind. The first step is not the weeding, or even the planting, but the vision of the gardener or the artist.

What do we want to achieve? This chapter is about the vision we have for our relationship. How do we change from two individuals into a couple?

To help see the process by which two separate individuals become a couple, we can find some suggestions in the research in social psychology. Psychologists tend to divide the formation of intimate relationships into different stages and recognize that certain qualities are necessary to move from one stage to another. Not all agree on the number of stages or their duration, but in general, we can use the following scheme. The first step is that two people have to come together. This is due to proximity (they meet somehow) and attraction. Undoubtedly, it is physical attraction that captures our interest and motivates us to pursue knowing the other person better. This is the chemistry that sparks the fire. This is the magical quality that stays at an unconscious level. It is a fascinating step and includes infatuation and passionate love, but it takes more to progress beyond this point. A next step is finding common interests and activities. There is a saying that states, "Birds of a feather flock together." Traditional research of the fifties and sixties found that most people who have stable and happy marriages are similar in many aspects. On average, people married someone who lived within a twelve-mile radius from their home and who came from similar cultural and religious backgrounds. Most also chose someone with the same socio-economic status who had similar interests and hobbies.

Many researchers believed that substantial differences within the couple were a risk factor for future dissatisfaction and separation. More modern research has confirmed much of the initial studies, but it has also refined it somewhat. We find that differences in ideas or habits that are not important to the couple have little impact on satisfaction. For example, if they have differing political views but neither one really cares about politics, then this difference will not divide the couple. As families are more mobile today and cultural and ethnic differences are more tolerated in society, these factors become less important in couple satisfaction, according to more recent studies.

Social studies have been less clear regarding personality similarities. Many studies indicate that it is in personality characteristics that "opposites attract." Many people end up marrying someone completely unlike themselves. The introvert is attracted to the extrovert, the dominant to the submissive, the easy-going to the driven, or the optimist to the pessimist. Whereas most studies confirm that this is an important aspect of our attraction to our spouse, research is mixed about the results on stability or happiness of the couple over time. Many studies have found that people with personality similarities are more satisfied. It seems that initially we are attracted by these differences, but with time, they can strain our rapport.

This research indicates that marriage or a relationship is easier when we come from similar backgrounds and similar experiences. This does not mean that if we do not, our marriage cannot survive. Possibly, it is not so much how similar or opposite we are but how we handle our differences that is important. Certainly, though, the more differences there are, the more misunderstandings and conflict there may be.

For example, I am American and my wife, Fernanda, is Italian. There are definite cultural differences between us. Not only this, but we disagree on just about everything. I like modern furniture and she likes antiques; I like sunny weather and she enjoys the rain; I like rock and roll, and she listens to rhythm and blues. I wish she would stay home and she likes to work. In addition, we are definitely opposites in personality. I am introverted and she is social and extroverted; I am a pessimist and she is an eternal optimist. The list could go on. We have certainly had our fights, but maybe because we have been aware of many of these differences from the beginning, they have been the reason for our having created better communication skills and having learned from each other, rather than being constantly divided. As a result, many similarities may help a rapport, but they are not necessarily essential to continuing the relationship. Instead, all research agrees that there are two important similarities that are necessary for the relationship to grow and progress. The first is having similar values, and the other is working toward common goals.

VALUES

The Merriam-Webster Dictionary defines values as "something (as in principle or ideal) intrinsically valuable or desirable."[1] In other words, these are the principles or ideals to which we ascribe the most worth in our lives or that which we most desire. These make up our philosophy of life. These are our most important beliefs. They may be part of our religion, but they do not have to be, and certainly, they encompass more than just religious belief. They define who we are. They also define what our priorities in life are and will be. Examples include our religious beliefs, our love for our families, nature, sports, or success. They include what we consider good character traits, like our work ethic, honesty, fidelity, and loyalty. These values will dictate what choices we will make. Is it more important to be honest, or should we compromise to have more success? Is my wife my first priority, or will I compromise that for temporary pleasure and satisfaction in extra-marital affairs? These beliefs involve just about everything we do. If these are fundamental aspects of who we are, why is it that so many couples have never sat down and shared these ideals? Why do we spend so little time reflecting on our own values? Most couples think that they share similar values and are rather shocked along the way to find that this is not necessarily true. Try writing down *your* seven most important values and ideals and then put them in order of priority. You may use the below list of different personality characteristics and values to decide what is most important to you. Pick the seven that you value the most.

Empathy, honesty, love, mutual communication, sincerity, desire for knowledge, righteousness, respect, fun-loving, achievement, peaceful, nurturing, sense of humor, confidence, faith, trustworthiness, responsibility, charity, goodness, family oriented, adventurous, hospitable, courageous, humility, greed, resourcefulness, enthusiasm, initiative, cleverness, style, rationality, emotionality, logic, intelligence, peaceful, friendliness, morality, passion, creativity, supportiveness, compassion, meekness, spirituality, energy, inspiration, charm, social graces, altruism, arrogance, zeal, decisiveness, self-sufficiency, neediness, integrity, cheerfulness, being laid-back, driven, tidiness, neat, cleanness, purity, attractiveness, capable, proud, understanding, career-oriented, dedication, inventive, thoughtful, studious, warm, people-oriented, task-oriented, education, faithfulness, loyalty, love of nature, spontaneous, and so forth.

To put these in order, first write on a sheet of paper the seven you think are the most important, whether from this list or from your own ideas. Then take any two and compare them. Is love more important than respect? If it is, then you can compare this to the next item on your list and so on until you have created a hierarchy from what is most important to you to what is least. Now write them down.

My ideals and values:

1.

2.

3.

4.

5.

6.

7.

Now, try writing down right now what you think are the seven most important values and ideals of your spouse.

My husband's/wife's values and ideals:

1.

2.

3.

4.

5.

6.

7.

Now verify your list with your spouse. Have him or her go through the same list and the same exercise of putting his or her ideals in a hierarchy. Did you guess correctly what his values are? How many of these values are similar? How does this influence your relationship? Discuss these with your spouse.

In conflict situations, differences in opinion, outlook, or personality can be overcome and can even be a stimulation to further growth. This is not as easy for differences in our basic values. If I love children and want a family and my wife is only interested in her career and perceives children as an obstacle, how do we solve that? I can wait, hoping that she will change her mind; I can sacrifice my ideal; I can impose my belief and values on her, but it will be difficult to ever find a win-win solution. A fun way to see value conflict in practice is to solve the following value puzzle with your spouse. This is taken from *Parent Effectiveness Training* by Dr. Thomas Gordon and is called "The Alligator River Story." Read the story and then list in order from best to worse (or from bad to worse!) your opinion of each character. Let your spouse read it separately and write his or her own list.

Once upon a time, there was a woman named Abigail who was in love with a man named Gregory. Gregory lived on the shore of a river. Abigail lived on the opposite shore of the river. The river, which divided the two lovers, was teeming with man-eating alligators. Abigail wanted to cross the river to be with Gregory. Unfortunately, the bridge had been washed out. So she went to ask Sinbad, a riverboat captain, to take her across. He said he would be glad to if she would consent to go to bed with him preceding the voyage. She promptly refused and went to a friend named Ivan to explain her plight. Ivan did not want to be involved at all in the situation. Abigail felt her only alternative was to accept Sinbad's terms. Sinbad fulfilled his promise to Abigail and delivered her into the arms of Gregory.

When she told Gregory about her amorous escapade in order to cross the river, Gregory cast her aside with disdain. Heartsick, she turned to Slug with her tale of woe. Slug, feeling compassion for Abigail, sought out Gregory and beat him brutally. Abigail was overjoyed at the sight of Gregory getting his due. As the sun sets on the horizon, we hear Abigail laughing at Gregory.[2]

Was your answer that the worst was Ivan and the best Slug? Or is Abigail the worst? Discuss it with your mate. Do not keep on reading until you discuss this with your spouse and come up with the same list.

What are the problems you had? Did you agree? Were you able to persuade your spouse that you were right? Why not? When this exercise is done by a group of couples, some heated discussions usually arise. Rarely does everyone agree. We choose these characters according to the values we have, and the differences in your list and that of your spouse show the differences in your value systems.

The important aspect of this exercise is not solving this story, but rather discovering how you resolve value conflicts. When people's values differ, all they can do is explain themselves and communicate why they feel that way. When they do this, their mates can understand each other's reasoning and where they are both coming from. They can explain themselves, and they can understand each other. But often they have to agree to not agree. For resolving the problem of Abigail, this is not very important, but when it concerns the principles that we value the most, it is. This is why it is important for couples to discuss these values before committing to marriage.

I cannot imagine sharing my life, sharing my innermost feelings, or opening my soul to someone who does not share my values. Fernanda and I are different in almost all aspects, but what profoundly binds us together are the values we share. The values we have are part of the compass that guides our course during our marriage. It is what keeps us on path when life's difficulties obscure the way.

FORMING THE WE

If you were paddling a canoe together, the important thing is that each paddles in the same direction. In marriage, if each has a different goal, they will always be in trouble.[3]

—Paul Popenoe

One of the most difficult transitions in relationships requires two individuals to become a couple. We have to move from me to we. We have to become a spouseship, not two individuals. The concept of spouseship or teamwork is essential to a lasting relationship. If two people cannot learn to work together, they will tear the relationship apart. Fortunately, because teamwork is essential in sports, business, and the military, a lot of research has been dedicated to understanding what makes a team work.

What transforms a group of individuals into a cohesive unit? Does a sports team win just because they have the best athletes? That surely helps, but there are other, more important factors. Often in basketball, football, or soccer, teams that were favored to win because they had the best players fail miserably. Why? Somehow, they did not create a team spirit that unified the players. They played with many talented individuals but not as a team. The same is true in creating a film, working on a business project, or being in a military unit; the whole is more important than the parts. It is the atmosphere and feeling that the director can create with both the star actors and the whole cast that will determine the success of the film. The unit has to work together. The player who always shoots the ball to increase his statistics, and is in competition with his teammates, will destroy the team. The businessman who uses his coworkers to look good and obtain the promotion will eventually destroy the motivation of the department. The soldier who strikes out on his own and does not obey orders can produce fatal consequences for his whole unit.

No coach wants to squash the individual talent of his players. It is not to limit the potential of the individual that the team is created but rather to enhance the potential of all the players. In business and in sports, this is called synergy. Synergy is defined as "joint action of different or discrete agents in which the total effect is greater than the effects when working independently."[4] In other words, synergy develops when people working together as a team produce more and better quality work than they could have done working alone. For couples it means that each person can create more, make more progress, and be happier together, than they could alone. This is a spouseship.

The following are three steps to creating a team spirit.

1. Common goals

Have you ever thought about what makes the difference between a "couple" and two people living together? What is the difference between a "family" and a group of people living under the same roof? These are questions that I often ask my classes when discussing intimate relationships. What is your answer?

Love does not consist in gazing at each other but in looking together in the same direction.[5]

—Antoine de Saint-Exupéry

The many answers that I receive are varied, but most students conclude that the basic difference is that a couple or family has common goals or objectives. They work together to create something. If this is a fundamental aspect of being a couple, it is surprising that so few couples have ever pondered or discussed just what their goals and objectives are, not only as individuals but also as a couple. What are the factors that bind two people as a couple? What binds you to your mate? What are your goals as a couple or as a family? Where are you going in life?

To find out, first list some personal goals that you have for your life.

My Personal goals:

1.

2.

3.

4.

5.

Now stop and think about what you want from your relationship. What are you and your spouse striving to create? What is your vision for yourselves as a couple? What are your common goals? List a few of these.

Goals for my relationship:

1.

2.

3.

4.

5.

How do your relationship goals differ from your personal goals? Do you believe that your spouse has the same goals that you do? Have you ever discussed these goals? Have your spouse write down his or her personal goals and relationship goals. Now compare your lists. Do you have the same goals? Are there conflicts between these relationship goals and your personal goals or those of your companion? Which goals have priority?

Certain issues that are extremely important to discuss early in relationships are those that have the potential to change the balance of power in the relationship. Each spouseship is based on sharing power equally. If only one spouse works or if one makes much more money than the other, how can the finances be handled so that the other spouse does not feel underprivileged or left out? If both have careers and one has to transfer to a new location, whose career takes priority? How important is it for one or the other to get ahead in their career? Are they doing it for the welfare of the family or for their own gratification? If both are working when the children are born, how will you handle this? Does the mother quit her job? Do you share the duties and both take part-time jobs? Do you send the child to day care when he is six weeks old, a year old, three years old, or in kindergarten? Do you both agree with this? It is essential that you talk together, that you discuss in depth your vision of the relationship from the beginning. It is surprising how many couples have not even talked about something as important as having children.

If you don't know where you are going, it doesn't matter what road you take, or how long the journey lasts.

—Anonymous

Part of this process of deciding your direction and deciding where to go with your relationship depends on the basic values that you listed previously. These make up your moral compass and indicate the direction you should take. Your goals should follow this compass, and together they create your vision for how you want to live your life. You must begin with your idea of what you want to achieve. When you have meditated at length and made decisions about where you want to go, this has to be discussed and agreed upon with your spouse. It is *your* relationship and you have to decide *together*. It is important that you write these goals down. Write down your vision as a couple for what you want to achieve together in your relationship and what type of couple and family you want to become. Stephen Covey, in his book *Seven Habits of Highly Effective Families,* calls this a mission statement and lists some questions that the couple may want to ask themselves:

- What kind of spouses do we want to be?
- How do we want to treat each other?
- How do we want to resolve our differences?
- How do we want to handle our finances?
- What kind of parents do we want to be?
- What roles (earning, financial management, housekeeping, and so on) will each of us have?
- How can we best relate to each other's families?

- What traditions do we want to keep and create?
- What intergenerational traits or tendencies are we happy or unhappy with, and how do we make changes?
- How do we want to give back (to the world, to society)?[6]

The fundamental issue is that you discuss together what you want your life to be like as a couple and later as a family. What is your vision of life? Take time tonight or sometime soon to begin this discussion. Look deep inside yourself and seek the vision of life that you want. What are your goals as a couple?

You've got to have a dream if you want the dream to come true.

—South Pacific

I cannot stress enough the importance of writing down your goals, your values, and your vision or mission statement. Frame it, hang it on the wall, and consult it often. You and your spouse should be consciously aware of where you are going and what your vision is for your life. It has been found that only about three percent of people actually write down their goals, but it has also been found that these are the most successful people in life.

If one advances confidently in the direction of his dreams and endeavors to live the life which he has imagined, he will meet with success unexpected in common hours.[7]

—Henry David Thoreau

When I met Fernanda, one goal that we both had and decided on was that we wanted a family with several children. We both wanted to further our education, and we wanted to travel. We both shared the goal of having a certain amount of economic security, with primary focus on owning a house someday. You can see that some of these goals are contradictory, because it is hard to further education and have children. It is even harder to do both and have economic security, much less travel the world. We had to prioritize these goals. In first place was, and still is, our goal to always be there for each other and to make our relationship and our family our number one priority, never letting the outside world and life's problems get between us and divide us. We are still working on this, and if we succeed in just this, we will have accomplished the most important goal of our lifetime. (We hope to still have time to travel since that ended up in last place!)

As you grow and change, you may find a need to modify your goals. As you reach some of the goals, you will want to look forward to new summits to conquer. It is like the mountain climber who reaches the top of the mountain only to see new mountains and peaks to strive for. You may not reach all of your goals as a couple, but you will have plotted the course that you want to take in life, and you will have created the relationship that you desire. Can we ask for more?

2. Enhance Each Other's Potential

Once you have worked together to create a vision and establish goals that you share and treasure, it is easier to put in second place some of your own individual aspirations because you can achieve more as a team than you can individually. You are no longer in competition with your mate. But you are working together for something that transcends each individual. When you do feel in competition, it is time to go back and share your common vision.

A second important aspect of teamwork is that each member of the team be aware of his role and of the roles of all the other players. Not everyone on a soccer team can score goals and be the hero, and not everyone can be a quarterback in football. But each player's role is equally important for the team effort. The truly great players like Larry Bird and Magic Johnson in basketball, or Pelé or Platini in soccer, are those who enhance the performance of the other players. They spark the energy of synergy so that the whole team plays better. The same is true in relationships. How is this achieved?

In sports, all the great stars lead by example. They are the first to arrive at practice, they train the hardest, and they push themselves the most; by doing so, they earn the respect of their teammates. They look to themselves and their improvement first. If the team loses, they do not blame others but ask themselves how they can improve. Then, they are sincerely interested in the welfare and improvement of their teammates, and support their efforts. They are never slackers. They do not sit back and let their teammates take over—they lead by example.

Which Are You?

There are two kinds of people on earth today;
Just two kinds of people, no more, I say.

Not the sinner and the saint, for it's well understood,
The good are half bad, and the bad are half good.
Not the rich and the poor, for to rate a man's wealth,
You must first know the state of his conscience and health.
Not the humble and proud for in life's little span,
Who puts on vain airs, is not counted as a man.
Not the happy and sad, for the swift flying years
Bring each man his laughter and each man his tears.
No, the two kinds of people on earth I mean,
Are the people who lift, and the people who lean.
Wherever you go, you will find the earth's masses
Are always divided in just these two classes.
And, oddly enough you will find too, I ween,
There's only one lifter to twenty who lean.
In which class are you? Are you easing the load
Of overtaxed lifters, who toil down the road?
Or are you a leaner, who lets others share
Your portion of labor and worry and care?[8]

—Ella Wheeler Wilcox

What does this poem mean for a relationship? Are you a slacker or a leader? Are you a lifter or a leaner? Are you giving one hundred percent to the relationship, or are you holding back to see what your spouse will do? One piece of advice that the temple president gave my wife and me at our wedding that I have found to be precious was, "Never do just fifty percent of the work in the relationship. Always do at least eighty percent of what needs to be done. Never wait for your spouse to ask your forgiveness, but make sure that you are always the first to start the peace process." It was not until later in my study of psychology that I understood why this was such good advice. We all suffer from what is called *Egocentric Bias*—that is, we overvalue what we do and undervalue the efforts of others. We know that it takes us great effort and sacrifice to get out of the chair and change the baby because we have had a long day and are tired, but we do not take into consideration that it is an equal sacrifice for our wives to cook dinner. What I perceive as my fifty percent of the chores and duties is really only thirty percent because I have overvalued my efforts. At the same time, the fifty percent that my spouse does seems to me to be just barely thirty percent because I will also tend to underestimate her contribution or take it for granted. As a result, almost all couples regularly do the thirty percent that they perceive is their part and argue over the remaining forty percent that no one is doing, each believing that the other is a slacker. If I set my sights for at least eighty percent, it is likely that I will succeed in doing at least my fifty. This is true for the division of labor, the chores that have to be done, taking care of the children and so on, but it is equally true for the emotional aspects of the relationship too.

Christ stated this even better: "And whosoever shall compel thee to go a mile, go with him twain. Give to him that asketh" (Matthew 5:41–42). Use this principle in your marriage. The first mile is what is required of you. This comes from a well-known habit in the Roman army in Christ's time. A soldier could oblige a man or boy to carry his pack, but only for one mile. This was so common that many boys had a stake driven on the side of the road to signal one mile from their home. Thus, they would carry the pack to the stake and then dump it, not taking it an extra step. Christ is asking us to do more than we have to—to go the extra mile. If we do this for others, shouldn't we do this even more readily for our eternal soul mate? Always do more than is expected, and always do it with a smile and in good humor, and your marriage will prosper.

Ask yourself: Am I doing everything possible to emotionally support my spouse, to lighten his or her load, to enhance his or her abilities, to calm him or her, and make him or her feel appreciated? Who makes up after a fight? Who listens more? What could you improve? How could you lead by example to make this a better spouseship? How can you deepen your relationship, progress together, and become soul mates? When things go wrong, do you first ask, "What could I do better? How can I improve so that our spouseship can improve?" This is the sign of a star player. Ask yourself daily, "How can I be the best spouse there is?" If you do this, you will have a successful, fulfilling relationship.

Bear ye one another's burdens, and so fulfill the law of Christ.
—Galatians 6:2

3. Common Heritage

The last aspect necessary to establish a team or spouseship is having a common heritage. The military has always been aware of this. Each unit in the military has its own name, insignia, banner, and history. When a soldier enters the unit, he becomes aware that he is part of a long and distinguished tradition, that others have preceded him and died for their country. He is proud to belong to that unit and feels part of that tradition.

He wears the uniform and the insignia that identify the unit. Each mission undertaken by this unit produces new experiences that are added to its tradition. Sports teams do the same. When a person becomes part of the LA Lakers, he is playing on the same team that has seen such great stars as Jerry West, Kareem Abdul-Jabar, and Magic Johnson. He wears the team colors and plays in the same stadium. He is part of a long tradition. He is also part of a new team that will add to that tradition.

As a couple, you are not isolated or independent but part of a long tradition that lasts hundreds of generations. You are not alone but part of a family history. You each have an ethnic and cultural heritage that is part of you and that you bring to the relationship. Whether you are aware of it or not, this tradition will have a profound influence on how you perceive the world and how you relate to each other. This book will mention the deep influence our family of origin has in our communication patterns, style of loving and arguing, and self-perceptions and ideas. The more we are aware of these influences, the more we can mitigate their negative aspects and take pride in the positive.

American culture has lost contact with its roots in many ways. Not only have we lost our family, ethnic, and cultural background, but also we are often physically separated from our parents, grandparents, and relatives and so lose that precious family heritage. Think how different it is in Italian and European countries where children often live in the same home that has been in the family for centuries and stay in the same town that has been seen dozens of generations of their family. Their parents still live nearby, as do their grandparents and relatives. They are immersed in family history. They have family traditions to live up to; they are aware of their origins. This gives the couple stability and continuity. They are not alone but are part of a long history of couples and families who have struggled, worked, and survived. They have developed farms, crafts, and professions, each generation trying to give something more to the following one. The couple is part of a team that has been going on for centuries. Possibly the problem of the European couple is that they are too immersed, and it is hard to become a separate unit. Certainly, though, the typical American couple loses much of its family tradition and sense of purpose.

It is important that we reconnect with our families and heritage to understand who we are as individuals and as couples. It is also important that we create our own traditions. Most marital therapists realize the importance of these family influences and often will begin therapy not with the couple but with their families. Without understanding where we came from and how we are influenced by family perspectives, we rarely understand the present conflicts.

There are many ways that you can connect with your past. Begin a family history by doing your genealogy—not just recording names and dates but finding out what were and are your family traditions, recipes, activities, and so on. Try asking your parents, grandparents, and other living relatives to record a history of their lives. Have them talk about their parents and their families. This is an exercise that I use in one of my classes, and students grumble about it, but most thank me later for making them reconnect. Many have had powerful emotional experiences as they learned how their parents and grandparents have overcome hardships and life's difficulties. Most find out that they knew little or nothing about these family members, even their own parents. It is a way of finding strength and courage when hardship occurs, knowing that those who preceded you have faced similar trials and have overcome them. It gives you family pride that carries on into your relationship.

In your relationship as a couple and later as a family, it is equally important to establish your own traditions and memories. These may begin with a videotape or photo album of your marriage and can continue with photos, scrapbooks, and memorabilia. It can also include small things like how you celebrate Christmas or other holidays, where you go on vacation, or sports or activities that you do together. Keep a family diary in which you record these memories, or keep copies of Christmas letters in which you relate the year's events. There are many computer programs now that allow you to organize and record these memories.

One of the traditions that Fernanda and I have established is our summer vacation. We both love the mountains, and since the beginning of our marriage, we have always taken vacations to the mountains of Italy, Austria, or France. There we take walks in the forests, hunt for edible mushrooms, identify the wildflowers and trees, pick wild strawberries, blueberries, and raspberries, and picnic on the mountainside near the crystal clear streams coming from the glaciers above. We used to hike up to the top of the mountains with our children in backpacks, but now as we age, we are content to take the ski lifts to the same peaks. We have collected ski patches from all over the Alps that we've sown onto our family backpack. We have passed this love for nature and for the mountains on to our children. They are all expert mushroom hunters even though two out of three do not even like eating them. This is something that defines us as a couple and as a family—it is part of the heritage that we pass on to our children.

As the forsythia and Japanese peach blossom gradually grow together and intertwine, they generate a new beauty. However, they are not the whole—they are only part of a larger garden. When the gardener plants new flowers or shrubs in the garden, she cannot just look at how they are today but must envision how they will become—how high they will grow, how they will coordinate with other plants in the garden, and how their colors will enhance the whole garden. So too, when we become a couple, we create a new entity, different from two individuals. We become part of a larger garden, and we need to create a new vision for ourselves. We are no longer two separate people but one.

NOTES
1. Merriam-Webster Dictionary (New York: Simon & Schuster, 1974).
2. Thomas Gordon, *P.E.T. Parent Effectiveness Training; Instructor's Guide* (Solana Beach: Effectiveness Training, Inc., 1989), 8–20.
3. Quoted in *Quotationary* (NovaSoft, 1999).
4. Merriam-Webster Dictionary (New York: Simon & Schuster, 1974).
5. Antoine de Saint-Exupéry, *Wind, Sand and Stars*, 1939. Quoted in *Quotationary* (NovaSoft, 1999).
6. Stephen R. Covey, *The 7 Habits of Highly Effective Families* (New York: Franklin Covey, 1997), 161.
7. Henry David Thoreau. Quoted in *Quotationary* (NovaSoft, 1999).
8. Ella Wheeler Wilcox, *Poems* (London: Kessinger Publishing, 2003).

Rule 4

FORGET THE FANTASIES

And ye shall know the truth, and the truth shall make you free.
—John 8:32

And truth is a knowledge of things as they are, and as they were, and as they are to come.
—Doctrine and Covenants 93:24

Have you ever noticed that almost all the famous fairy tales deal with relationships, and most have the same theme? Think of Snow White, who is the most beautiful damsel in the land. Her beauty causes envy. She has to escape and finds refuge with seven dwarves. She is finally discovered by the wicked queen but is saved in the end by the handsome prince. It is love at first glance, and they live happily ever after. On the other hand, think of Cinderella, who is also beautiful, envied, and hidden, not by dwarves but amongst the dirt and ashes. The prince discovers her, immediately falls in love, and so magically transforms her. It is *instant* love, but he has to diligently search her out. Sleeping Beauty shares the same story line, containing a beautiful maiden that has to be found and saved by her Prince Charming. It is *instant* love, and they live happily ever after. Maybe Beauty and the Beast changes the theme somewhat since it is the lovely maiden who has to discover the hidden good in the beast and transform him, much like the princess who transforms the frog with a kiss. Still, they all lived happily ever after.

In all these stories, the exciting part of the relationship occurs during the courting period and has to do with discovering the beautiful maiden or handsome prince and being transformed by love. Note that the woman is always the most beautiful in the land, and the man is always handsome, powerful, and rich—a prince. Love occurs instantly and without any real effort, and they always live happily ever after without any further effort. After a childhood spent watching these shows and hearing these stories, is it any wonder that people, young and old, have unrealistic expectations about relationships?

There is a formula that states, Satisfaction = Reality / Expectations. In other words, I will be happy if my everyday reality compares favorably to my expectations. There is no better way to spend your life unhappily than to believe the fairy tales. They raise our expectations to unrealistic heights to which reality can never correspond. The formula is not quite accurate in that it suggests that a simple solution would be to keep your expectations so low that anything in reality would be better. If you expect to be beaten, humiliated, and abused, then reality is usually going to be much better. Low expectations, however, in either others or ourselves, make us lose our hope and enthusiasm for life and lead to depression, not happiness. The solution is not low expectations but realistic expectations.

In fact, many studies indicate that the one factor that will most influence our satisfaction in marriage or in any relationship is how realistic our expectations are. We all have expectations about our spouse, about marriage, about family life, about the roles of men and women, and about our future. These expectations shape our perception of marriage and the world around us. In turn, our perceptions play an important part in whether we feel fulfilled, joyful, and happy, or whether we are frustrated and depressed.

This is true about everything in life from school to work to free time, but nowhere else does it seem that our expectations are so off-base as in intimate relationships. In one study published recently a team compared the expectations of young adults toward many negative life experiences such as the probability of having a car accident, cancer, heart disease, bankruptcy, and divorce. In all of the categories except divorce, these people had realistic expectations that corresponded with national statistics. But only 12 percent believed that their relationships could end in divorce even when they knew that statistics indicate that first marriages among the young have a 64 percent chance for divorce.[1] We somehow believe that love will conquer all and that our relationship will never fail. The problem is that these expectations are often unconscious. They are secretly hidden away in some corner of our minds. Even when we are disappointed, rarely do we look inward and analyze our expectations to see if we began with realistic perceptions. Also, just as rarely are these perceptions and expectations very realistic. We are equally prone to these fantasies whether or not we are members of the Church. The purpose of this chapter is to present some of the most common misconceptions or fantasies and give indications about how to recognize them and eliminate them before they ruin our relationship.

The process of creating expectations originates through socialization and culturalization. This process begins at birth and includes not just what our parents and society tell us but all the subtle hidden messages that we unconsciously absorb from both. The two main sources of this process today are the family of origin and the media. In the family of origin, we observe and absorb, without ever really thinking about the process, communication patterns, problem-solving skills, emotional reactions, gender roles, acceptable expression of affection, discipline methods, and much more. These are somewhat modified by later experience, but much of our primary socialization remains as a unconscious measure of how relationships *should* be, and I emphasize "should." Once we internalize these beliefs and attitudes, they become, in our minds, what is right and proper. Anything different from these behaviors is, therefore, wrong and improper. A brief example will illustrate the nature of this socialization and show how it can create communication problems in a relationship.

Jane comes from a family that is quite affectionate and emotional. There is a lot of hugging, kissing, and physical display of affection. Her parents are also quite emotional, particularly her mother. She has seen that when they fight, her mother screams, yells, and maybe throws plates, but that afterward they make up and there is physical display of affection again. John instead comes from a family where logic rules. There is little display of emotions, and affection is expressed mostly verbally. When his parents disagree about something, they tend to withdraw, pout, and reason things out. They then reunite, maybe a few days later when the emotions are under control, and reason together to solve the problem. In his home, his father is dominant and usually is able to control the situation. Both of these families are functional, and both sets of parents would say that their marriage is satisfactory.

Jane is attracted to John because he seems so logical, and she knows that this would help her reign in her emotions. John is attracted to Jane because she is so spontaneous. They have a wonderful romance, and John is swept along by the passion of love and feels, maybe for the first time, the warmth of physical affection. All goes well until after their marriage when they have their first big fight. What is going to happen?

Yes, Jane is going to rant and rave and carry on, shouting and crying, and John will be totally taken aback by this behavior and will withdraw. The more he withdraws, the more Jane will feel hurt and will react even more emotionally until John finally escapes, slamming the door. John will pout for a few days, and Jane will feel devastated. Each of them is secretly arriving at the conclusion, "My spouse doesn't love me." Jane will feel that if John really loved her, he would respond to her and shout back, and then they could passionately make up. She is disconcerted by his cold, unfeeling attitude and feels unloved. John, on the other hand, feels that Jane is completely out of control and should seek therapy. He feels that if Jane really loved him, she would keep her emotions under control and seek a rational solution to the problem. He feels equally unloved, because now any attempt to rationally solve the problem sets off another emotional outbreak in Jane.

Both John and Jane feel unloved, and what is tragic is that both were actually behaving in a loving way according to their model of love. Jane was acting out what she had unconsciously absorbed as loving behavior from her family, and John was doing the same. Just about anyone in a relationship can think back to the first few fights and probably remember similar miscommunication. John and Jane may be two extreme examples of communication and fighting behaviors, but on the other hand, they both came from "normal" and "happy" families. What about all the children of the many dysfunctional families today in America? What styles of communication and affection have they learned? What will happen when they enter a relationship?

Step 1: Recognize the triggers that indicate that unrealistic expectations might be in place.

We saw in the episode above one of these triggers, such as the feeling of disappointment in our spouse or bewilderment about how they act. The thoughts that "if he really loved me" or she "should" or "should not" do certain behaviors are indications that you are thinking in absolutes. You are thinking that your way is "right" and all other ways are "wrong." Other triggers come from our family of origin. The sooner you discover what you absorbed unconsciously from your family and the patterns that your mate also learned, the sooner you can recognize your own triggers. It is our own personal truth about how things are and how they were that will set us free from bad habits, unrealistic thinking, and the "traditions of our fathers."

Try this exercise to see what you learned from your family. Think about it and try writing down what the communication style of your parents was. How did they resolve fights? How did they show affection and love?

How much does this influence you today? What is your style? How close is it to theirs? Now examine your spouse's style. Have your loved one do the same exercise with his family. Now try writing down his communication style, how he shows love and how he shows anger. How much comes from his family of origin?

Some people after the first fights start looking at and questioning their own reactions; others do not unless they begin therapy, and most never do. The tendency is to accept our way as normal and remain terribly disappointed in our companion. Our expectations have encountered another disappointment. We may even attempt for years to change our mate to conform to our standards and expectations. The Book of Mormon repeatedly explains that the Lamanites hated the Nephites because of the traditions of their fathers. These traditions, handed down from one generation to the next, distorted their perceptions of the Nephites and caused hate, envy, and wars that lasted centuries. This is how powerful these expectations can be. They can only be changed by confronting our ideas with the present reality.

Thus, a major source of our unconscious expectations comes from our family of origin, and these differ from one family to another. There will always be some differences between husband and wife about how to express love, how to communicate, and what the gender roles are, because no two families are the same. The fantasy is that there is just one *right* way to express love, or to solve problems—our way. Any other way is the *wrong* way!

Step 2: Examine yourself. What are your expectations? Are they realistic?

Once you start recognizing your triggers, stop and examine yourself. Every time you feel disappointed by your spouse, stop for a moment and ask yourself why you feel so disappointed. What were your expectations? Were they realistic? Does your spouse share them? Begin a discussion with your spouse to find out what your spouse thinks and to explain your expectations and perceptions. Every time your spouse does something that just doesn't seem right, ask yourself if he or she is thoughtless and selfish or if he or she is working on a different set of rules. Is your way the only way to look at this?

We talked about the fact that self-honesty is the hardest kind. Self-examination of our own perceptions and expectations is just as difficult because these perceptions become the filters that we use to see the world, and we do not see the filters. Instead, we judge and criticize our spouse.

The Lord had much to say about this habit:

> Judge not that ye be not judged. . . . And why beholdest thou the mote that is in thy brother's eye, but considerest not the beam that is in thine own eye? Or how wilt thou say to thy brother, Let me pull out the mote out of thine eye; and behold, a beam is in thy own eye. Thou hypocrite, first cast out the beam out of thine own eye; and then thou shall see more clearly to cast out the mote out of thy brother's eye." (Matthew 7:1–5)

It is interesting that the Lord is clearly saying that we judge others according to our imperfect perceptions (the beam in our eye) and that we must clarify our own misconceptions before we can assist our spouse. The purpose of this chapter is to introduce some of the common misconceptions, "beams," or fantasies that people have so that you can identify yours.

Another attitude or set of expectations that originates in the family of origin has to do with the satisfaction of needs. Children are by nature dependent and demanding. They have many needs that they are unable to fulfill on their own. They need love—both emotional support and physical affection. We need to nurture them physically, emotionally, socially, and intellectually. The paradox of parenting is that the more we satisfy the needs of our children—the more we are able to love them and give them that sense of security—the less demanding they are as adults. That is to say, the more the parents give and sacrifice for their children, the more the children learn to give and sacrifice. The more the child feels loved and treasured, the more he or she will be able to share love with others. By loving them, we do not spoil them. By satisfying their needs (not their wants!), we give them the sense of security and trust necessary for them to form stable, loving relationships.

Unfortunately, none of us are perfect parents, nor did we have perfect parents. All people come away from childhood with unfilled needs and seek to fulfill those needs with a spouse. As long as we have also learned to give and nurture, this does not create conflict because we receive fulfillment from our spouse and are able to give them love and support.

Many people, however, never received the proper nurturing, have deep unfulfilled needs, and unconsciously expect their spouses to satisfy those needs while lacking the ability to reciprocate. Their spouse becomes their parent. Particularly in times of stress, they are only able to take and not to give. The more a child was deprived of love and affection, the stronger his needs are and the less capable of loving he is. This will continue unless he finds someone who is very caring and generous with love, someone who can satisfy his needs and teach him to give.

At times all of us unconsciously expect our spouses to take charge, be the parent, and let us be the dependent child. When we clearly communicate to our spouse that we need a break and they help us, this is quite acceptable. More often, instead, we unrealistically expect them to read our minds and understand exactly what our mood is and what they should do for us. Often we do not understand our problem, but we expect our spouse to do so. When they do not even notice our mood or do not understand the problem, we are greatly disappointed, and we feel misunderstood and unloved. When this happens repeatedly, the disappointment grows, and we lose our trust in that person. Often, however, the spouse was quite willing to nurture. He or she just did not know how to satisfy that need or even what the need was. It was the expectation that was unrealistic, not the spouse who was unloving. A simple example might clarify this.

I came from a family in which my mother suffered from severe migraines that became more frequent with the passing of the years. She would often remain in bed for two or more days with the blinds shut and would not move or eat. We learned as children to move quietly about the house and to fend for ourselves during those periods. I unconsciously learned that if someone is sick, you leave that person alone—you stay quiet and fend for yourself. In general, as a child, I learned that when something happens, you accept it and try to make the best of things. My wife, Fernanda, came from a home that was much more proactive about health and about everything else. She absorbed the concept that if something is wrong, you fix it. Therefore, if someone is sick, you take him to the doctor, you make him herb tea or chicken broth, and above all, you comfort him.

In the beginning years of our marriage when my wife was sick, she would go to bed, and I would leave her alone and quietly fend for myself. Rather than explaining her needs, she was hurt and disappointed in me and bewildered by my actions. To explain my behavior to herself, she elaborated all sorts of theories about how I was in denial about illness or how I only loved her if she was strong and healthy. Unfortunately, it took years before we finally communicated about this. Since then, I bring her chicken broth and comfort her even though it does not feel like the right thing to do.

The fantasy is that we will find someone who will take care of us, nourish us, and satisfy all our needs. We secretly desire our spouse to be the perfect parent whom we probably never had, and we are hurt and disappointed when our spouse does not live up to this fantasy. It is rarely rational, but it can be a powerful impediment to a happy relationship. The more unrealistic our expectations are, the more negative perceptions we have about our spouse and our marriage, the more unhappy we will be.

Step 3: Communicate—Discuss your perceptions and expectations with your spouse.

We usually look at the world through our own individual filters and we are not even aware that we have them. It is like having sunglasses on and when you come out of the sunlight, everything seems so dark and distorted. This sensation will remain until someone reminds you to take off the sunglasses. Then, all of a sudden, the world brightens. Our spouse is the person who can best see that we still have our glasses on and who can help us see more clearly. This can only happen when we open up the discussion and comment on our perceptions. When we tell our spouse that we perceive something negative in our world, then together we can identify if the problem is the glasses we are using or if something is really wrong. In the words of Dr. Phil:

> We all view the world through individual filters—our personalities, attitudes, points of view, our "styles"—powerfully influence the interpretations that we give to the events of our lives; those interpretations in turn determine how we will respond, and therefore how we will ultimately be responded to.[2]

In the same book, on page 113, Dr. Phil relates an interesting experiment done on a group of conservative elderly ladies from a local Baptist church. First, they were hooked up to sophisticated polygraph-type equipment that registered any variation in their bodies' physiology. Then they were shown a series of stimulus words that ranged from totally ordinary and neutral words like *oak tree* or *stagecoach* to words that were offensive and obscene. When the neutral words were presented even for exceedingly brief intervals, the ladies were able to perceive and report them without errors. When the offensive words were presented even for ten times the length of time of the neutral words, the ladies overall did not respond to them. Their perceptual defenses filtered out these words so that they did not consciously hear them and could not respond to them. They did not flinch; they did not blush or show any outward sign that they had heard these words. Unconsciously, instead, the physiological reaction of their bodies went haywire each time with significant alterations of their heartbeats, breathing, skin temperatures, and so on. Their unconscious was definitely reacting to what their conscious mind did not or would not see. What is the consequence of this? In the words of Dr. Phil:

> Thus, on one hand, the perceptual defense mechanism protected these ladies' conscious values and beliefs; on the other hand, it also created a huge hole in their view of the world. Your perceptual defenses have the same effect on you. When you see the world like a censored letter, with 50 percent of the words cut out, you are living a fantasy. . . . Your "blind spot" may be the very things in your life that you need most to see. A scary thought![3]

This *is* a scary thought. Let your soul mate help you fill in the "blind spots" that you have. Let him or her help you take off your glasses and see the world a brighter and better place. You can only do this if you open up with love and trust and discuss your perceptions and expectations.

Closely connected to the expectation of having our needs satisfied is the idea of who takes care of whom—who does the work. This expectation also originates in the family and results in how we divide gender roles and chores in the home. Not long ago, this division of labor was mostly dictated by social tradition. Men took care of the relationship outside the family and "manly" chores. Thus, the husband paid the bills and dealt with taxes, lawyers, or any relationship with authorities. He mowed the lawn, took out the garbage, and shoveled the snow. The wife had jurisdiction over the household. She cooked, sewed, cleaned, did the laundry, and took care of the children. These roles were so entrenched that for many years, once women started to work outside of the home, they continued doing all the household chores too. There was very little conflict because each spouse knew what was expected of each other; they had seen their parents do it. All accepted it.

As social evolution changed our perceptions of what men and particularly what women are capable of doing, this modified our expectations in the home. The problem is that there is no new set of established roles; each couple has to negotiate and divide the labor between themselves. This sounds easy—a contract is made early in the marriage, usually a verbal agreement, and each person's chores are spelled out. Instead, this division of chores often goes against entrenched perceptions and expectations, particularly in the male. Usually the chores that were traditionally male were also duties of higher social status. Thus, the women felt left out or underprivileged.

This is particularly true for work outside the home, which gives the woman economic and social status. The chores of women instead were seen as low status, or busy work. Therefore, men have little incentive to take over these chores. They were often brought up in a home with traditional roles, and although they may rationally acknowledge that it is only fair that since their wife works they should share the household chores, *it still does not seem right.* The perception he has, maybe unconsciously, is that it is not his job, and he is making a concession to his wife.

Many men still refuse to do much in the home, particularly with the children. One study found that in American households where both spouses worked but there were no children, totaling up the number of hours between career work and household chores, it came out about equal with the man dedicating fifty-eight hours a week and the woman sixty. In the households with working parents and children, however, it became highly disproportional with the man still at about fifty-eight hours but the wife and mother spending seventy-two hours a week.

In many cases, even when the man does the household chores like washing the dishes or doing the laundry, he has the distinct perception that this is a big favor for his wife. It is something extraordinary that he is doing for her, something that she should deeply appreciate. Women contribute to this because unconsciously they feel that this is still their domain. Therefore, often we find that the husband washes the dishes, but the wife will later criticize the job, not because he did not clean them well, but because he did not do it "the right way," which means her way.

Working out who does what in a relationship seems like a fairly banal point, but many marriage manuals consider it one of the fundamental factors as to whether a marriage will function or not. Rationally it is easy, but most of our perceptions about who we are as males and females and what a male or a female does are part of that unconscious baggage that we carry from our family of origin. It is part of our self-esteem. It also has to do with our unconscious needs. For example, I know of several men who get quite upset because dinner is not ready when they get home from work. This is true particularly if their wife does not work outside the home. This is not because they are famished and if they do not eat, they will suffer. In fact, often they cannot really explain it. Once they examine it, what is really going through their heads is, "If my wife really loved me, she would prepare dinner for me." Rationally, they may acknowledge that this does not follow, but internally, part of their perception of their wife's role is that she prepares the dinner. Undoubtedly in their family, Mom showed her love by doing these chores. This is what seems right to them; this is their expectation. They may learn to cook for the family or fend for themselves, but it will never seem "right" to them.

These expectations do not concern just household chores but things like who initiates sex, who takes over in a crisis, who pays the bills, and many other aspects of family life. These differing expectations lead to much of the conflict that every couple encounters in the first years of the relationship. Another example that demonstrates how most of these expectations remain unconscious is given again by cohabitation. Frequently two people who have lived together without major conflicts for years decide to finally marry. They have proven to themselves that they are quite compatible. They marry, and then, soon after, they begin fighting. What was peaceful coexistence before now becomes a battleground. What is strange is that they are both bewildered and baffled by this. What changed? In appearance, nothing has changed, but under the surface, they have now triggered a whole new set of expectations. In cohabitation, each did his or her part and expected very little of the other. Now, however, the woman is the wife and the man expects her to stop seeing other males, or the man is the husband and the woman wants him home at night. All those expectations unconsciously absorbed during childhood now come out and everything changes. They are now constantly disappointed with their new spouse, and they don't understand why. The whole relationship has changed. This is another reason that a marriage after cohabitation has less of a chance for success than if the couple never lived together.

These differences in family upbringing and the resulting expectations are the reasons communication skills are so necessary for a successful spouseship today. The good thing is that if the proper verbal skills exist or are learned, many of these differences can be discussed and negotiated. First, however, must come the realization of what our unconscious expectations are.

Step 4: Behave lovingly even if it does not feel like the right way to do things. You need to communicate in the language of love of your spouse.

Once your mate has communicated to you what love means to him or her and how he or she wishes us to express it, to continue doing what you have always done because you think that it is the only "right" way is to ignore your spouse's needs. This does not show love. Do it their way. Express your love according to what feels right to your spouse.

SOCIAL FANTASIES

Now, what about the fantasies and perceptions that the entire culture creates and that both spouses unconsciously share? What happens when we are both wearing the same sunglasses? For example, all of us were raised on the same fairy tales. Dr. Kinder and Dr. Cowan in their book *Husbands and Wives: Exploding Marital Myths* state that one of the major reasons half of the married couples in America end up divorcing is the false expectations and myths that people have or come to believe about the marriage. Here are some of the myths that they mention:

1. Marriage will always make you feel complete and whole.
2. Your mate should change for you if he or she really loves you.
3. If you truly love each other, passion will always flourish.
4. Differences should always be negotiated.
5. If you're not feeling fulfilled, your marriage must be at fault.
6. If you have to "work" on a marriage, something is wrong.[4]

American culture has many fantasies about relationships, but we will discuss just some of the more common.

PASSIONATE LOVE

Many who read the first chapter and the discussion about what love is and is not were probably quite disconcerted. Love, particularly in an intimate relationship, is part of our cultural upbringing. That is, it is so much a part of our thinking that we rarely question it. Because everyone in the culture grows up with the same idea and it is thoroughly ingrained in us, we do not think about it.

In American culture, for example, love and marriage are associated—we marry because we are in love. Hollywood, romance books,

Cosmopolitan, and the media in general all portray love and romance with emotional turmoil, sex, lust, and wild jealousy. It is overwhelming. In my psychology classes, we often do an exercise in which we list all the qualities of passionate love on one side of the board and what we commonly called companionate love on the other. Before reading on, try listing for yourself the qualities of each.

Passionate Love	*Companionate Love*
_____	_____
_____	_____
_____	_____
_____	_____
_____	_____

Under passionate love, we find terms and ideas like lust, chemistry, physical attraction, sexual desire, emotional roller coaster, and exclusiveness—where we cannot think of anyone except our spouse. We have butterflies in our stomach, depression, jealousy, and so on. On the other side with companionate love, we have friendship, trust, commitment, trustworthiness, respect, reciprocal esteem, reliability, and intimacy. Students then look at this second list and say, "How boring!" In fact, few consider this love at all.

Countless books, movies, and TV shows have ingrained in us that true love is sexual, passionate, and emotional. It gives a high, and if it does not, it is not love. For this reason, we "fall in love," and when this high emotion ends, we say, "I have fallen out of love." It is something that happens to us, requires no work, is extremely satisfying, and is something we would like to go on forever. It can happen at just about any age, and it makes us feel alive and happy. The one thing that all researchers agree on, however, is that it does not last. It is short-lived, sometimes a few days, often a few months, and rarely more than a year or two. Most cultures define this as infatuation and excuse the adolescents who experience it, knowing that it will not last and knowing that it has little to do with marriage.

American culture instead has idealized passionate love to the point that if you are not feeling passionate and sexual every day of your relationship, something is wrong. If you are no longer feeling these strong emotions, then you have fallen out of love. If you no longer have butterflies in your stomach each time you see your spouse, it is all over. If you do not desire each other sexually each time you get together, you are no longer in love.

Almost sixty percent of teenage marriages end within two years. Why? The couple falls passionately in love, they get married within months, and they fall out of love within a year. They realize their mistake and they divorce.

This is not an attack on passion or even on passionate love. Passion is a natural physiological response of our body. It heightens our awareness, increases our mood to the point of euphoria, and therefore is extremely pleasurable. Its purpose is to begin the mating process. Passionate love constrains us to focus almost exclusively our energies and attention on the other person, to feel sexual attraction, and to desire to be together. We can use this increased energy and attention to learn to know the other person, to exchange ideas and intimacy, and to build trust and commitment. This can be, and often is, the first step to establishing a lasting love that will endure a lifetime and all eternity. But it is not an end in itself—it is not the love of soul mates.

If this energy and desire remains only lust and is used exclusively for passionate sex, very little remains for creating friendship, sharing ideas, or working toward goals with the other person. Yet these are the elements that will determine whether a relationship will work. When two people can commit together to resolve problems and work on goals, they gain knowledge about one another and learn to depend on each other. This creates the trust necessary for an ongoing relationship.

Therefore, passionate love can be an exciting first step, but that is all it is. It is not sufficient for a lasting relationship. Otherwise, we would be like most animals that pass from one mating experience to another, seeking the thrill of the hunt, the conquering, the submission, and the sex. Many people in fact pursue just this, convinced each time that they have found true love and are incapable of going further. Instead, to find the true joy and satisfaction of an enduring relationship, couples have to find ways to sublimate this energy and desire so that it can transform into a form of companionate love. It is a misconception that companionate love is passionless and no more than friendship. As we will see, there is and should be passion and romance, but this is not the primary focus—it is not what exclusively binds two people in a meaningful relationship. It is just one way of expressing love. True love, instead, is the uniting of spirits and the sharing of inner feelings in a climate of trust and commitment.

Intimacy is a spiritual spouseship that has to be based on trust. I cannot open up my deepest feelings, thoughts, or emotions if I do not totally trust my spouse. If I can't share this part of me, the most personal, intimate part, then my spouse will never really know me, nor will I know her, because it has to be a reciprocal process. If she does not know me to my core, then does she really love *me?* If I cannot share my feelings, even my negative feelings, then she loves only what she can see in me. What is special about a true relationship of soul mates is that the couple can be totally themselves and therefore loved for who they are. We need someone who can see through the dirt and rags to our inner beauty or who goes beyond our frog-like appearance and brings out the prince. If we cannot do this, we will never feel truly loved. This only happens with time and trust. We open up a little at a time and test the other to see their reaction. As we see them open up, we open and share more until we both can express our inner thoughts without fear that our spouse will trample them. Passionate love may begin this process, but more often than not, it may even impede intimacy, because we focus only on sex.

The fantasy that our culture has created is that true love is always passionate love with fireworks and sex. It is chemistry and we are helpless victims swept along by the passion. We are "in love." The film, book, or fairy tale always ends with "they lived happily ever after." This is the love that the Greeks called madness; it is not the true love of enduring relationships. Often it is not love at all. They will *not* live happily ever after if they do not create trust, commitment, friendship, and intimacy.

EFFORTLESS ACHIEVEMENT

A second fantasy shared in our culture is a corollary of the first. Since love just happens by fate or by chemistry and just as mysteriously disappears, I am not responsible. It takes no effort on my part to be in love or not be in love. Therefore, when I have fallen out of love, it still is not my responsibility or my fault; it just happened. Or, even more likely, if it is not my fault, then it is my spouse's fault.

This sets us up to believe that I cannot do anything to prevent this, nor am I responsible. So, we search for love again in a new mate, find the passion and lust again, feel alive, and then watch it all go sour. Many people repeat this process over and over, passing through multiple relationships and many marriages, convinced each time that they have found love, and each time getting disappointed. They never learned that relationships require work.

Work is love made visible.[5]

—Kahil Gibran

The fantasy even reaches the point that many people believe that if they have to work at it, it is not love. Since love is spontaneous, then it must be effortless. Thus, if they have to make an effort, it is not love. We challenged this assumption in the first chapter. If we redefine love as service, as doing something for the other person, then it is clear that effortless love is only a fantasy. Love is the opposite of selfishness. When we are selfish, we satisfy our desires and needs first. When we love, we satisfy the needs and desires of our mate or children first. It is evident that most of the effort of love is overcoming our own selfishness. We all know that a tree that is not pruned will not bear fruit, and so it is with people. What tree, though, if given the choice, would cut its own branches? Overcoming selfishness is much the same. It is difficult to use self-control and self-restraint and to put others first. This, however, is the replacement of love.

Step 5: Become aware of the social messages that bombard you through friends, books, films, advertisements, magazines, and other media. Rationally examine them to see if they are a realistic view of relationships and love. Does your parents' marriage or the relationship of any of the people you know personally resemble the fairy tales?

Another fantasy that our culture has perpetuated is that marriage will automatically make a person happy. Hollywood and the media have brainwashed us to believe that we have a right to happiness and that this is a natural and enduring emotional state. We feel we should always be happy. Therefore, if we are unhappy, something is wrong—something is out of order from the natural state of affairs. One evidence of this desperate search for happiness is that anti-depressants like Prozac are the number-one selling prescription drug in the United States and Europe and that chronic depression has tripled in the last fifteen years and now affects forty million people or more in the United States alone. Because we do not feel happy, we seek artificial means to happiness.

One of the ways society tells us we can be happy is in a passionate relationship, so we seek out someone who will make us happy. Since in a relationship I should now be happy, if I am still unhappy, it must be the other person's fault. Therefore, I should leave that person to find someone else to make me happy. More and more the media displays that it is not the relationship but rather the good sex in the relationship that gives us joy. Therefore, we are now looking for passion and sexual compatibility, not companionship and friendship. This explains a marriage contract that states that I can leave you because you gained ten pounds. You are no longer sexy. You are no longer stimulating. Society also explains that I will be happiest when someone fulfills all my needs, so the purpose of a relationship is to find someone who will fulfill all my needs.

To many people, this will sound perfectly natural. So where is the fallacy? First, happiness, like the emotions discussed in chapter 1, is ephemeral—it comes and goes. In no one is it an enduring state. Second, it is not certain. The constitution states that a basic right of all people is *"the pursuit* of happiness," but no one has guaranteed that you will achieve it or that it will remain once found. Third, and most important, it is a personal responsibility. *No one else can make you happy.* Your perceptions and expectations will cause your happiness or unhappiness. All studies have found that happy people have happy marriages and that unhappy people are unhappy in their relationships too. *No one else can make you happy.* Even if your spouse does everything possible to make you feel loved, you can still interpret this as something negative. Our emotions are under the control of our thinking process, which is influenced by our perceptions. In the end, how we perceive the world, our mate, and ourself determines our happiness. In large part, our expectations create our perceptions, whether they are realistic and positive or unrealistic and constantly disappointed. I repeat: *You are responsible for your own happiness!*

Step 6: Take responsibility for your own emotions. Whenever you blame your spouse for your unhappiness, you are wrong. Any time you say to yourself, "I am disappointed or unhappy because of my marriage," you are shifting the blame. Go back to step 1 and start the process again.

Finally and most important, the more enduring emotion of joy or satisfaction is not achieved through fulfilling our physical needs but through growth. If you think about it, satisfaction and joy come to you when you learn something new, when you accomplish a difficult task, or when you help someone else. It often requires sacrifice and dedication, but this is what truly fulfills you as a person. In this sense, relationships do cause joy and happiness because they are learning and growing experiences and they allow us to serve one another.

For even as love crowns you so shall he crucify you.
Even as he is for your growth so he is for your pruning. . . .
Love possess not nor would it be possessed;
For love is sufficient unto love. . . .
Let these be your desires . . .
To wake at dawn with a winged heart and give thanks for another day
of loving;
To rest at the noon hour and meditate love's ecstasy;
To return home at eventide with gratitude;
And then to sleep with a prayer for the beloved in your heart
And a song of praise upon your lips.[6]

—Kahil Gibran, *The Prophet*

LDS couples are not immune to any of the above fantasies and are susceptible to additional myths that members of the Church commonly believe that are dangerous for their relationship. Let us mention just two.

The first false expectation is based on a true principle that is poorly understood. As members of the Church, we believe in a spirit life before coming to this earth, or a pre-mortal life, in which we created friendships and relationships that endure here on earth. We believe that often we were predestined to come into our family and to meet a spouse that we already loved to create our own family. This is the true principle. One misconception is that many believe that anyone with whom they fall in love is always that one special person, whereas this may not be true. We can be fooled by our own emotions. The false expectation or myth, however, is that once we have found our soul mate, everything will work out, we will always love each other, and we will be together because it is destiny!

A second false expectation similar to the first is that if we find a worthy member and marry in the temple, then *automatically* the marriage will go smoothly because we are both on the same wavelength, and we are both trying to live gospel principles. Certainly, this is a good base for a marriage. Everyone should strive to fulfill this covenant, but it does not guarantee that there will not be misunderstandings, conflicts, and disappointment in the marriage. Unfortunately, many marriages in the Church begin in happiness and bliss but do not endure the trials of time and the adversities of this life. The principles are the same whether you are a worthy member or not; it is the truth that will set us free, not fantasies.

It is interesting that Doctrine and Covenants section 93, which explains the nature of truth and light, is the same section that advises us that we need to continue from grace to grace until we receive a fulness of knowledge. The process of examining our own false perceptions, unrealistic traditions, and irrational reasoning lasts a lifetime until we can have "fulness." Our beloved mate is our most precious friend in uncovering our own defects and false beliefs, so instead of resenting our spouse when they show us the error of our thinking, and resisting their suggestions, we should have the humility to be thankful for their aid. Together we should seek the light of the Spirit that suggests truth to our souls.

> For behold, thus saith the Lord God: I will give unto the children of men line upon line, precept upon precept, here a little and there a little; and blessed are those who hearken unto my precepts, and lend an ear unto my counsel, for they shall learn wisdom. . . . Cursed is he that putteth his trust in man, or maketh flesh his arm, or shall hearken unto the precepts of man. (2 Nephi 28:30–31)

Any gardener knows that maintaining a beautiful flower garden takes hours and hours of labor. It is not enough to trust to the sun and the rain. The earth has to be turned and nourished. The water has to be given regularly, and the weeds have to be pulled. The plants themselves often have to be pruned and trimmed or they will overgrow their roots and not produce flowers or fruit. Within months or a year, an abandoned garden will be overgrown with weeds and lose its original beauty. The same is true of a relationship. It takes constant nourishment, pruning, and effort. Problems and conflicts like weeds have to be eradicated, and new ones will continue to creep up. Injections of the fertilizer of new experiences has to be provided, and a steady dose of the water of communication is necessary, or the plants will wither and die.

NOTES
1. B. Flowers, E. Lyons, K. Montel, and N. Shaked, *Journal of Family Psychology,* March 2001. Quoted in *Monitor on Psychology* (APA, March 2001).
2. Phillip C. Mc Graw, PhD, *Life Strategies, Doing What Works, Doing What Matters* (New York, Hyperion, 1999), 155.
3. Ibid, 113–114.
4. Melvyn Kinder and Cowan Connell, *Exploding Marital Myths, Deepening Love and Desire* (New York: Signet Books, Reissue Ed., 1990).
5. Kahil Gibran, *The Prophet* (New York: Alfred A. Knolpf, 1967), 30.
6. Ibid, 12–15.

Rule 5

VALUE THE DIFFERENCES

For all have not every gift given unto them; for there are many gifts and to every man is given a gift by the Spirit of God. To some is given one, and to some is given another, that all may be profited thereby.
—Doctrine and Covenants 46:11–12

Where there is no difference, there is only indifference.[1]
—Louis Nizer

No two people are alike. We are all different. This is what makes life interesting. We saw several examples in the last chapter about how we unconsciously absorb values and behaviors from our family of origin. We do the same from the school environment and all the experiences of our lives. These form us into unique individuals. Although we all know and would agree with this, we are still frequently disconcerted at how different we really are. In everyday life, we tend to look more for similarities and ignore most of the differences. It seems we even have an inborn tendency to believe that other people are like us and share our views.

Each person tends to overestimate other people's behavior that is similar to their own. We do this for two reasons. One, because it builds self-confidence. If others believe and act as we do, this reinforces our confidence that our own actions, opinions, attitudes, and lifestyle are normal and appropriate. The other reason is that we tend to associate with people who are similar to us, who have the same hobbies, interests, and beliefs, so we tend to overestimate the number of people who are similar to us. Because we associate with our friends and discuss topics that are of common interest, we come away with the impression that our friends are just like us. Often in the beginning of a relationship, particularly if founded on friendship, we may have this same opinion of our spouse. We are then astounded and often disappointed when we get to know them better and realize how different we are. They do not think as we do, they do not perceive the world in the same terms, and they often do not understand us.

One of the paradoxes of intimate relationships is that we are attracted to the other person because they have qualities that we do not and that compensate ours, but then once we are together, we wish that they were more like us. Many people spend a great deal of time and effort trying to change their spouse into someone like themselves.

We perceive any difference between our spouse and ourselves as threatening; thus, we become defensive and the arguments begin. We feel threatened because what we have always considered right and inviolate is disregarded or contradicted, and it requires us to re-evaluate our beliefs. This causes stress, and the easiest way, apparently, to lower the stress is to change our spouse. With the new spouse, however, nothing will change. All people are different and differences will create some conflict. We tend to see all conflict as negative, and conflict within a supposedly loving relationship as bad—as a sign that love has flown the coop. Society has insinuated into our minds another fantasy still: if it is true love, if it is a good relationship, there will be no conflict.

It is this concept, however, that is fundamentally wrong. If we view marriage or any lasting relationship as a journey toward fulfillment, as personal progress to becoming more actualized people, then we must realize that it is this contrast of opinions, this diversity of perceptions, and this difference in behavior that allows us to reexamine our position and grow. Any time there are differences, eventually conflict will ensue, but the solution is not to eliminate the differences but rather to learn to manage conflict in a positive way, which will be the subject of a later chapter. The first step, however, is to perceive the differences as positive. We must appreciate and value the differences between ourselves and our spouses as an instrument of personal growth and progress as a couple.

When two men in business always agree, one of them is unnecessary.[2]
—William Wrigley Jr.

One concept that we have already mentioned is *synergy*. Two or more people, when they join their resources, can create more together than they could as separate individuals. In marriage, this means that the couple together should be able to achieve more than either person could alone if they interact and work together as a unit. This does not mean that there is always harmony and never conflict. Dean Tjosvold, a management consultant, said:

> The stereotype that harmony and teamwork go together causes great damage . . . But positive conflict is a critical reason that teamwork has so much value. Teams (couples) have great potential in large part because they allow for diverse contributions and perspectives and forge them into an integrated approach.[3]

It is the differences that allow us to grow, be more aware of our strengths and weaknesses, and create positive synergy. The couple that uses their differences to pursue the journey and to better themselves will walk into the sunset "happily ever after."

> *By blending the breath of the sun and the shade, true harmony comes into the world.*[4]
>
> —Tao Te Ching

Too often, the differences divide and ruin the relationship. It is not the diversity but how we face it that makes the difference. Besides the individual idiosyncrasies of each person, there are many documented biological differences, reinforced by society, between men and women that exacerbate these feelings of misunderstanding. We will examine some of the major differences that generally exist between the sexes, the reasons they exist, and what each should value in the other.

MEN AND WOMEN

Have you ever questioned why women love flowers and seem more sensitive to body odor? Studies have found that women are far more sensitive in their sense of smell than men are. Some studies indicate that they are as much as seven times more sensitive. Therefore, I envy my wife, who can walk out the door and tell me what flowers are in bloom when I have to stick my nose next to a flower to smell its fragrance. She can also tell if I, or our sons, have been in a room where people smoke when we walk in the house.

Have you ever noticed or been amazed at your husband's ability to know just how to find a place that you only went to once, years ago? Studies show that men far outperform women in spatial orientation—that is, to know where you are in a maze, to mentally rotate objects in your mind, or to visualize a map.

These are just some of the biological differences found between men and women. There are others, such as women's verbal ability or men's capacity for abstract thinking. In all cases, these generalizations apply to some men and women but certainly not all. Rather than consider this as an either/or situation, we should see it as a continuum from woman to man in which the preponderance of each sex may vary in one direction or the other but never includes everyone. Let us examine what research has found.

In the sixties, brain research revealed that the two hemispheres of the brain, previously thought to have the same functions, specialize in different tasks. The left hemisphere, besides controlling the right side of the body, also controls our verbal, mathematical, and logical skills. In subjects whose brains had been divided so that the two hemispheres no longer "talk" to each other, when a simple math problem was presented only to the right hemisphere of their brains, the subjects were not able to solve it. If a picture was presented to the right brain, they could not describe it even though they could draw it with their left hand. The right brain is incapable of logic, analysis, and verbalization. It is more difficult to localize the functions of the right hemisphere, but it too has specialized capacities. It is now commonly known as the artistic or creative side, and this is true to a point. It has the ability to perceive patterns, to make sound and symbolic associations, and to see the relationship between the parts. It also contains the capacity of spatial orientation. We process many of our emotions on the right side.

Since in the normal person the two sides of the brain communicate constantly, these divisions do not seem particularly important. In the last fifteen years of research, however, we have found that the brains of men and women develop differently and that this brain lateralization may explain many of the differences commonly found between the sexes. The development of girls while in the uterus, including the brain, is a harmonious process. The template of nature is the woman. The two hemispheres of the brain grow at the same rate, and the tissue that connects the two sides, called the corpus callosum, is well developed. To develop as a male, instead, requires the addition of hormones produced first by the Y chromosome and then by the testes. This allows the development of the male sex organs but also affects the development of the brain. The brain is washed with high levels of testosterone in its early development, and this changes the growth pattern. It seems that first the right hemisphere grows, and then the left. In normal cases, the left hemisphere will remain quite dominant. The cells of the corpus callosum remain smaller and there are fewer cells, so that there appears to be far less communication between the two sides of the brain.

The prefrontal cortex also seems different in men, allowing them to shut out or ignore input, particularly emotional input, from the right hemisphere. Other areas of the brain are also affected, in particular the hypothalamus that later controls growth and aggression. When the left side of the brain is not dominant in the male, then the right side seems to be strongly in control, but there is rarely the harmonious symmetry found in the woman's brain. Robert Bly, poet and author, explains the connections between the two hemispheres as a "superhighway" of connections in women and "a little crookedy country road" in men.[5] This is an apt description.

Overall, there are far greater differences between the brains of men and women of all races, countries, or ethnic groups than those between these groups. That is, there are few differences between the brain of an American man or a Chinese male, no matter how different their life experiences are, or between an African woman and a European woman. Nevertheless, there are many differences between a woman's brain and a man's brain, and we can see these in the specific abilities that each sex has.

There are other major differences too, particularly in our sensory perceptions. Because women concentrate more on patterns and are more interested in people, they are better at recognizing faces and remembering personal information. They have a better sense of hearing. They can locate the origin of a sound more quickly or accurately than males. Six times more women can sing in tune than men can, and this begins in early childhood. They are more sensitive to tone of voice. This is why they react more strongly to someone who raises his or her voice. They discern emotional content from the tone of voice that most men miss completely. As said, women have a better sense of smell and are up to seven times more sensitive to smells than men. Thus, women are more sensitive to both the fragrance of a flower and the stink of body odor. Men are more sensitive to salty taste and prefer it, and women are more sensitive to sweets. Men have better depth perception and better focused vision, but women see better in the dark and have more accurate peripheral vision.

Women react more quickly and accurately to pain but have greater resistance to long-term pain. The greatest sensory difference between the sexes is the sense of touch. Women are so much more sensitive to tactile stimulus that there is almost no overlap at all with men. As a result, they react to touch more—it is soothing, and they will tend to touch, to soothe, more. Women need to be touched more, and they thrive on physical closeness. It is said that every woman, in order to stay in emotional balance, needs to be touched, held, caressed, or hugged at least twelve times each day. If men could learn just this one lesson, it would greatly improve the harmony of their relationships.

Even in memory skills there are differences. Men tend to have better memory for information that is organized logically and in context. Women have better memories for random and seemingly irrelevant facts. They organize information differently than men. Women tend to remember personal information and relationship connections far better. For men these have little context. For example, in one experiment, students were asked to wait in a small room with a cluttered desk while the experimenter went to "get things ready." The students thought they were simply waiting for the experiment to begin, but this was the experiment. After two minutes, each student was brought to a separate room and was asked to describe everything he could remember from the room where he had been waiting. Women in general were able to describe the room in great detail—the colors, the furniture, and even most of the objects on the cluttered desk. Men, on the other hand, could remember little or nothing. Whereas women organize these items using associations in the right hemisphere, men have to see a logical connection to organize memory. On the other hand, they have better skills for abstract thinking. Although there are few differences in math skills among younger children, in adolescence, with the introduction of algebra and abstract math, boys excel. For every exceptional woman in the field of higher math, there are thirteen exceptional males. Engineering and math are still heavily male dominated, whereas in almost every other college faculty, women are more numerous.

FUNDAMENTAL DIFFERENCES THAT YOU SHOULD VALUE

> *Who can find a virtuous woman? For her price is far above rubies. The heart of her husband doth safely trust in her. . . . She will do him good and not evil all the days of her life.*
> *Strength and honour are her clothing; and she shall rejoice in time to come. She openeth her mouth with wisdom; and in her tongue is the law of kindness. She looketh well to the ways of her household, and eateth not the bread of idleness.*
>
> —Proverbs 31:10–12, 25–27

Let us examine some of the major differences that exist, keeping in mind that this is still a generalization. There are men and women who do not fit this mold, but the majority do. Those that do not still often marry men or women who are opposites. That is, often men who do not fit this mold and have many of the characteristics of right hemisphere thinking marry women who are very logical and left hemisphere thinkers or vice versa. Another thing to keep in mind is that the brain is a constantly changing organ, and therefore some of the skills that were weak to begin with can be improved with practice and stimulation.

We will examine just three major differences between the sexes and then what we should value in our spouse. It is difficult to separate one quality from another because they tend to cluster together, but these are the central qualities.

1. Men are goal-oriented, women are relationship-oriented.

Men tend to be left hemisphere dominant and therefore will be very analytical and logical. They tend to focus on facts, figures, and concrete elements. They are oriented toward objectives, can focus their energy to achieve goals, and are able to exclude emotional elements in reaching the objective. This ability to reach objectives is part of the desire to conquer and to be in control. All these qualities can be positive if they are not exaggerated. This is what allowed the male to be the hunter. He could focus energy on reaching the objective, overcome many obstacles to achieve the goal of finding the prey, and kill the animal without emotional involvement. He would be a poor hunter if he saw Bambi in every deer he shot and had guilty feelings about it. He could travel great distances without becoming lost because of his ability for spatial orientation. This is still true of modern men even though the objective is no longer the hunt.

This is something that a woman can and should admire in her husband. Give him a goal, and he will focus on that to the exclusion of everything else; he will focus his energy on the objective and keep the couple or family focused too. He is not easily thwarted by obstacles and does not allow emotional considerations to interfere.

If, for example, a couple wants to buy a house and needs to save money for that, let the man establish the budget and do the savings. Make sure that he knows what else has to be in the budget, or he will let his children dress in rags and eat just hot dogs to accomplish his objective. But he will arrive.

The female, on the other hand, has a brain in which both sides are in constant communication. She has an ability to perceive relationships and associations that the male misses, because they take place on the right side.

This hemisphere perceives patterns, makes non-logical associations, and understands symbolism and relationships. This is just as true for poetry as it is for people. Together with her ability to perceive emotional expression, she becomes an expert on relationships, including her own. She is interested in people and what they do, and remembers personal information about people she knows or cares about. My wife remembers the ages and even the birthdays of people we barely know. She even remembers their children, when I can hardly remember my own. The woman has a better memory of personal facts, and she will remind you of just what you said, your tone of voice, and how you hurt her in an argument ten years ago!

The woman knows intuitively when something is wrong in the relationship and will initiate the process to improve it. In marriage counseling I often ask the couple to evaluate their relationship on a scale of one to ten. I always ask the husband first, and usually he will say seven or eight. The wife will then look at him amazed, and exclaim, "Seven or eight? We are at best a four!" She knows the relationship is suffering and usually is the one to bring the couple into therapy. After years of studying relationships in school and doing therapy, I am still amazed that my wife can see others' relationships far more readily than I can. This is even truer for our relationship.

Let your wife be the barometer of your marriage. Let her tell you how the relationship can improve. Use her innate abilities to teach you how to be a better spouse. Use her to connect to other people on a more personal and meaningful way. Admire her ability to relate and to improve relationships.

2. Women feel, men detach.

One of the main functions of the right hemisphere is to process emotional experience, particularly negative emotions. As a result, the woman who has the two parts of the brain in constant communication emotionally experiences all facets of life. Its emotional aspects color each fact or perception; she feels things! She can also readily verbalize these emotions. She is more interested in people and their feelings. She focuses on relationships more because she readily perceives interpersonal interactions and the subsequent emotions. She suffers negative emotions and depression more than a man does. Not only is she in contact with these emotions, but she is also better at seeing them in other people. Studies have found that women are far better at discerning facial expression than men are. From birth, baby girls gaze at faces longer and more intensely than boys do. They are also far more sensitive to tone of voice and can notice subtle differences in voice tone that men do not even hear.

For example, in one study, actors were filmed in a group who would display certain emotions requested by the experimenter. That is, on request, they would all show anger, happiness, fear, and so on. They then showed these films to couples and asked men and women to identify the emotion displayed by the actors. For some emotions like happiness, men and women were similar in their perceptions. Men perceived and reacted more quickly to expressions of anger, but the greatest difference was with negative emotions of sadness or depression. Women perceived these immediately, and many men did not perceive them at all. They saw normal expressions. Therefore, we find the common complaint of wives who say that when they feel down, their husband does not even notice. Often it is true—he does not.

Not understanding how emotions permeate all aspects of life for women, men are often taken aback by the wide range of emotions that women exhibit. They complain that their wives are too emotional and swing from one emotion to another. What they fail to understand is that this is one of women's most important attributes. This sensitivity to emotions allows women to not only tune into their own feelings but also to understand and be sensitive to others, including their spouses. It is because of this that women are sensitive to the needs of their children and can provide comfort and care. The male is not often in tune with his own emotions at all and has a hard time communicating his feelings. Often, he expresses all his feelings through the one left hemisphere emotion of anger. When he is frustrated, he gets angry. When he feels guilty, he gets angry. When he is depressed, he is grumpy. And sometimes even when he is excited he appears aggressive.

What the wife can do is teach her husband, through example and sensitive care, how to feel and express a broader range of emotions. He can learn to get into contact with his emotional side and become more sensitive to other people's emotions and feelings. It does not come to him naturally but he can learn. This is one of woman's greatest gifts to man and he should be grateful.

Because the prefrontal cortex in men seems to be more developed, this should be responsible for his emotional detachment. He tends to think more abstractly. Men use conversation to gather factual information.

Men gather facts, debate issues, and solve problems in a detached way, as abstract ideas. Deborah Tannen in her book *That's Not What I Meant!* calls this male tendency to communicate "report-talk."[6] Women need to relate issues to people. All issues have an emotional and personal content for them; they *feel* the issues. This detachment in men can create severe problems in the relationship because men detach from their emotions even on personal issues. The most common female complaint about their spouse is that he will not open up. He does not express his feelings. It is not that he will not, but rather he does not know how and needs to learn. This can be a negative trait at times when he should be sensitive and supportive, but it is also something positive. The woman can often become so involved in relationships and emotions that she becomes overwhelmed and cannot see any solutions. When something happens, she cannot sort out what to do and may feel helpless.

This is where the male can excel. He is emotionally detached from the problem and can see more clearly and find a greater number of solutions. He can put emotional problems into a better and more logical prospective. He can see the forest from the trees. He detaches and therefore compensates her involvement.

3. Men are concrete, women are expressive.

Men like to solve problems. They like puzzles, and they are good at solving problems of a concrete nature. They work well with facts and can abstractly manipulate the facts and details in their head to see many possible solutions. They take a logical, systematic approach to problem solving. They need the concrete facts. The male's communication style often follows this same logic. He likes to communicate facts and details. He is fascinated with statistics. He will often dominate the conversation, interrupting often to get more facts. He will often feel frustrated when his wife talks because she goes off on tangents. Her conversation is full of associations with one thing leading to another that he just cannot follow. His conversation will not be about relationships or emotions since these are foreign to him. He is not a good listener because he likes to jump in and solve the problem.

These skills together with those mentioned previously allow the man to excel in many jobs. The man conquers the problem and he enjoys it. He then feels useful. When a couple has practical problems to solve, the man can be quite effective, and it will make him feel needed and useful. The dilemma is that most of the problems within the home need people skills that he may not be adept at handling. One of the greatest needs that men have is to feel competent and capable—to be in control. In the workplace, they are able to use their skills and demonstrate their competence, and their co-workers and employees admire them. Then they come home and feel useless and criticized. Give your husband control over certain functions of the home, make it a competition, and he will excel. I clean the bathrooms at home. My wife has no say over how I arrange the shelves or how I clean as long as I do it. I then compete with myself to make sure that the bathrooms are cleaner than any other room in the house. It took me quite a while to figure out that I was dedicating a lot of time to a task I really did not like, but I still have to show her that I am as good or better at cleaning than she is. She has used my talents, and I feel competent and useful.

The same thing happens when a man expresses love. He tends to act concretely to show his love but does not express it verbally or emotionally. Often in therapy, a wife will complain that her companion never says that he loves her. When asked the husband is astounded that she has this view, and he will list the things he does to show his love. In one case, for example the husband told his wife, "Didn't I just take out a large life insurance policy in case I die?" For him this was a clear declaration of love; he was solving a potential problem. For her it had little or no meaning. Another typical scene is the couple that has seen little of each other the entire week, and finally on the weekend the man gets up early to wash her car. He does it to show his love, and yet she is thinking, "See, he doesn't love me; he would prefer being with the car rather than with me!"

Understanding the other person's point of view helps, but it is also important to communicate love and affection in a language that the other person understands. I can still remember my parents. Each time my mother would tell my father that she loved him, he would answer, "Ditto." A woman wants to hear, both verbally and nonverbally, that she is loved. She wants the love letter and the affectionate words and actions. A loving husband needs to provide these. He, however, needs the concrete actions of her attention for him—food and sex—all of which he interprets as expressions of love.

Women are more intuitive and spontaneous. They verbalize more than men and use associations that most men cannot follow. They solve personal problems by talking about them or listening while the other person expresses the problem. Researchers performed a study in which they attached microphones and recording devices to men and women over a period of weeks and calculated the number of words stated per day. They found that men on the average said about 12,000 to 15,000 words per day. Women, however, said about 18,000 to 24,000 words per day. Women talk more, sometimes twice as much as the average man. This begins in early childhood and continues throughout life. When a woman feels down or has a problem, she often finds solace by talking about it. One reason that women engage in therapy more often is that they are finally able to talk to someone about their problems and afterward they feel better. A man does not talk as much, does not talk about personal problems and emotions, and does not necessarily believe that he has solved anything by talking about it.

These differences often lead to some of the greatest misunderstandings between men and women. The husband comes home from work, and his wife has had a bad day with the children, or at the office, and starts telling him about it. She will tend to bring in peripheral information of who did what and why that he isn't able to follow, and he will interrupt, maybe with impatience, because he wants the facts to solve her problem. He thinks that she is asking him for advice, or asking him to solve the problem, when all she wants is someone to listen to her and give her emotional support. As a result, both feel frustrated, and she feels that he does not understand her or love her. She can short-circuit this negative process if she will tell him up front, "All I want you to do is listen." He then knows that he does not need to use his problem-solving skills, and he can relax and listen.

Men should appreciate and admire their wives' verbal ability. The relationship would be sterile without her ability to verbally express love and affection. He should learn from her capacity to express her emotions and become involved in relationships. Rather than be frustrated with her mental associations, he should be in awe of her ability to relate everything to the personal.

My wife can go on for hours talking about what happened at work, who said what to whom, and all the conflicts and jealousies that exist in her workplace. I have learned the names of about thirty people whom I have never met but about whom I know all sorts of personal information. I am always amazed at her ability and quite envious of it. I can usually sum up my day in one or two phrases: "Yeah, it was all right." This is not because I am not verbal but because I missed all these kinds of associations.

In intimate relationships today, women expect and demand a spouse whom they can talk to, express themselves to, and be understood by. They want a spouse who listens and is understanding and sensitive. These are qualities that men have never been trained to have.

If you think about it, women spontaneously have the abilities of both sides of their brain. They are then trained for years in school to use mostly left-hemisphere thinking. School trains them to think logically, use analysis, and solve problems. They can take this knowledge, coupled with their natural relationship and verbal skills, and become effective in both the workplace and the home. The male, on the other hand, has natural logical skills that are refined at school. But in what occasion in life does he learn to use the right hemisphere? When does he learn to verbalize emotions or even to perceive those emotions? When and how does he learn to focus on relationships? Who teaches him? The only person capable of teaching a man these skills is a woman, but many women do not realize just how incapable the man is, because these skills come naturally to them. The training hopefully begins in the home with his mother and must continue in life through his relationships with other women.

The brain is a wonderful instrument, and nothing is set in stone. We can learn new abilities constantly, but some come far more naturally than others can. Some skills require great effort. Therefore, men can learn to be sensitive and relationship-oriented if they want to and if they have a patient teacher. Women can become more goal-oriented and can learn to read a map. There will, however, always be differences.

The important question is, do we appreciate the differences? Do we value what our companion has that we do not? We will come back to these differences and explore more in later chapters how to resolve conflicts that may arise, but the vital issue is: do we value each other for who we are? Do we try to change each other into someone else?

Do these differences divide us, or unite us with synergy? Much depends on what each person wants to happen in the relationship. Are you threatened by new experiences or different opinions, or do they stimulate you to meditate and change your own beliefs and habits? These differences with your spouse should allow you to use them as a mirror to see yourself, your behaviors, and attitudes from a new perspective and therefore change. If you can perceive your spouse as the means for self-growth, then you are grateful for the differences. Otherwise you are just defensive and begin the conflict.

How does this relate to you? How is your mate different from you? Try thinking and writing down some of these major differences.

Now write a note to your mate and explain all the qualities that you most admire and value in him or her. Give your spouse a copy, keep one for yourself, and then every so often update what you have written by adding new qualities.

An interesting exercise that brings home these gender differences is suggested in the book *Relationships* by Dr. Les and Leslie Parrot:

> What if you were the opposite sex?
>
> Try imagining that you are your mate for a day, and keeping this in mind, answer the following questions.
>
> 1. What is your first reaction to living as the opposite sex?
> 2. How would the simple task of getting ready in the morning be different if you were the opposite gender (the time it would take, what you would do, how you would dress)?
> 3. How would living as the opposite sex affect your career choice and other aspirations?
> 4. As the opposite sex, would you feel more or less safe in society? Why?
> 5. Would you feel any different about your marriage if you were the opposite sex?
> 6. How would your relationship with your father and mother be different if you were the opposite sex?[7]

Compare these answers with your mate's. Come up with other questions on your own.

In any flower garden, it would be rather boring to find only red tulips or only blue and white petunias. Not only would it be boring, but also once these flowers faded, there would be nothing to replace them, and the garden would lose its splendor. It is by the variety of colors and contrast of plants that a garden reaches its beauty. It is because the forsythia is different from the Japanese peach blossom that each enhances the attractiveness of the other. If the forsythia insisted that the Japanese peach blossom have yellow flowers just like it, where would the splendor be? What would enhance the yellow of the forsythia? It is not by changing your mate that you make your relationship better but by appreciating your spouse's abilities, perceptions, and traits.

NOTES
1. Louis Nizer, *Between You and Me* (New York: Pyramid Books, Revised ed., 1964).
2. Dean Tjosvold, *The Conflict-Positive Organization* (Reading, Massachusetts: Addison-Wesley Publishing Co., 1991), 1.

3. Ibid, 154.

4. Ibid, 156.

5. Les and Leslie Parrot, PhDs, *Relationships* (Grand Rapids: Zondervan, 1995), 63.

6. Deborah Tannen, PhD, *That's Not What I Meant* (New York: Ballantine Books, 1986).

7. Les and Leslie Parrot, ibid.

Rule 6

SEEK THE POSITIVE

For where your treasure is, there will your heart be also.

—Matthew 6:21

The mind is a marvelous instrument, and one powerful function that it has is its "search and find tool." The mind will focus on what you direct it to find. Let us do a couple of experiments. Close your eyes and think of all the objects in your room that are blue. Now, open your eyes. What happens? If you are like the average person, when you open your eyes, it is as though all the blue objects in the room jump out at you. Try it again and think of orange, pink, or any color you want. The same thing will happen.

Another experiment we will perform used to enhance creativity is called "brutethink." Take any abstract idea, say freedom, and any concrete object, for example a pen, and think of the similarities between the two.

Even though these objects are two entirely different elements, the mind starts finding the similarities. For example, we can use a pen to write about freedom. Alternatively, freedom without the confines of responsibility is like the ink without the container—it is spilled and wasted; it dirties us. What did you think of?

This idea is expressed by Michael Mikalko in his book *Thinkertoys*:

> The human brain cannot deliberately concentrate on two separate objects or ideas without eventually forming a connection between them. No two inputs can remain separate in your mind no matter how remote they are from each other.[1]

Let us try another. Imagine that your challenge is how to improve relations with your husband or wife. Then you randomly select the word *pencil*. Try thinking of all the connections there may be between that challenge and a pencil. For example:

1. Eraser—We both keep bringing up past failures. We need to erase them.
2. Yellow—I do not have the courage to confront her. We need to have a sincere conversation about out finances.
3. Lead—Get the lead out. I need to stop being lazy in the relationship and letting things slide.
4. Six sides to a pencil—The six things that I need to work on in our relationship are . . .
5. You continue.

The purpose of this exercise can become more apparent in the next chapter, but in this case, it is to show the power of the mind. Our mind will elaborate upon whatever we put in there. Nevertheless, the famous saying from the computer industry, "Garbage in, garbage out," indicates that everything depends on what we focus our attention on.

Two stories better illustrate this point. A couple is going house hunting, looking for their dream house. They have visited many houses, but either the house itself, the surroundings, or the price is not what they want. Finally, they visit a beautiful house on a hill with a beautiful garden surrounding it and a magnificent view of the surrounding countryside. They are almost afraid to ask the price but find that it is within their means. Everything is perfect, but the wife is sure that there must be something wrong. Therefore, she inspects the house from the basement to the ceiling and comes back and says, "No, we cannot take it."

Astounded, the husband and the owner who has shown them the house ask what is wrong. "Is it the kitchen?"

"No," she says. "The kitchen is large enough and well organized, and has a window that looks out over the flowers in the garden."

"Is it the living room, then?"

"No, the living room is spacious with a fireplace and windows that look over the valley—it is just what I wanted."

"What is wrong then?" they ask.

"Well, from the pantry, if I stand on my tiptoes and lean to the left, I can look out the small window there and see the alcove where you store the garbage. I just could not live with that!"

Once there was a farming village in a wide, fertile valley. The village was near a forest that covered the nearby hills and mountains, but most of the inhabitants never ventured into the forest. The men and women were too busy tilling their fields and tending their cows and goats to have time for wandering in the forest. One man in the village, however, spent his life trekking in the woods, gathering healing herbs, chestnuts, mushrooms, and other plants from the woods that he would sell to the villagers. Whenever he returned from one of his trips into the forest, he would tell tales of the marvelous sights and adventures he had experienced in the forest. Or, he would speak of the beautiful flowers or unusual plants he had seen. Finally, after one of these stories, one of the villagers asked, "Why don't you bring us one of these plants?"

The next time he went into the woods, he came back with a beautiful wildflower that he carefully held in his hands. A group of villagers came near to look at the flower. One said, "But there are all those dead leaves on the plant!"

Another said, "Why did you bring it with all the dirt?"

Another joined in, "You pulled it out with a weed!"

The mountain man, rather disgusted, pulled off all the dead leaves and gave it to the first man. He pulled off the weed and gave it to the last, and then he shook the dirt off into the hands of the second. Shocked, they asked, "What are you doing?"

He replied, "You looked at a beautiful flower, and all you could see was the dead leaves, the dirt or the weed, and that is what I am giving you. I saw the marvelous colors of the flower and the delicate petals and that is what I am keeping."

Unfortunately, we often do what the villagers do or what the woman buying a house did. We experience something pleasant but find all its faults. We take something positive and turn it into something negative. The same thing is true of our relationships. We take the person who was the most precious in the world to us, and we start looking at all of their negative qualities. As we saw, the brain will focus on what we look for. Just as those blue or orange objects in the room jumped out at you because you were looking for them, so do the negative qualities of your spouse if that is what you want to focus on. Just like the lady who was willing to forgo a perfectly wonderful home because there were a few minor defects and she just knew that that was all she could remember or concentrate on later, so many people throw away a wonderful relationship because the other person isn't perfect.

Some people are never able to admire the unique beauty of the wildflower because all they can see is the dirt, the dead leaves, and the nearby weed. In the end, like the villagers, we get out of life and out of our relationship what we look for—what we focus our attention on. Which do you prefer: the flower or the dirt? The woodsman did not even see the dead leaves because he was so taken with the beauty of the flower.

Do not over analyze your marriage; it's like yanking up a fragile indoor plant every twenty minutes to see how its roots are growing.[2]

—Ogden Nash

Many studies try to explain why some relationships work out well and many do not. Psychologists have examined just about all aspects of the relationship, from communication styles, to sexual relationships, money problems, health, or any other types of problems couples face. These studies have not substantiated that any of these factors or others they have examined distinguish satisfied from unsatisfied couples. They have found that all couples have had similar difficulties and obstacles to overcome. The most common arguments are over finances, education of children, in-laws, the mother working or staying at home, or the frequency and quality of sexual intercourse. All couples go through these conflicts, so why are some overwhelmed and dissatisfied, and others overcome these problems, growing stronger?

The one difference is that happy couples laugh at past discussions. They may poke fun at their spouse's faults or at themselves but do not see each other as the enemy. They maintain a positive perception of their spouse as a companion, maybe full of faults, who is sharing the same journey.

In a recent study by John Gottman published in his book *Why Marriages Succeed or Fail,* Gottman extensively examined satisfied and dissatisfied couples and compared their different aspects, from personal background to personality qualities to economic standards. This research took years, and he found that even communication styles and sexual conflicts had little to do in distinguishing the two types of couples. He found that it all boiled down to one factor—positive messages. The satisfied couples exchanged more positive messages, whether through words, body language, or behavior than the dissatisfied couples did. He was even able to find that there is a critical number. There have to be at least five positive messages of approval or love and appreciation or respect for every negative message each day for a couple to remain satisfied with their relationship. Not only that, but the more positive messages, the happier the couple. Just diminishing the negative messages did not help that much; the positive has to be there.[3]

One key to a fulfilling and happy relationship is to focus on the positive aspects of your spouse and express appreciation, love, and admiration to him or her several times a day.

There is a reason that this is so important that relates to the brain and how we create memories. The brain does not passively store information; instead, it colors memories with cues from our surroundings, with our personal prejudices and beliefs, and with our emotions. That is why we link memories not just by logical associations but also by input from our environment and our internal emotional state. Scientists have found, for example, that students remember facts better if they are sitting in the same seat, in the same classroom, as when they first learned or memorized those facts. Even more important, they remember facts better when they are in the same mood or emotional state as when they first learned those facts. Psychologists label this State Dependent Memory, and it can be extremely important for relationships. This explains, for example, why depressed people can only think depressing thoughts. When they sink into that emotional state, it releases all their previous memories of failure or worthlessness, and positive memories fade and become meaningless. Only depressing thoughts come to mind.

If I argue with my spouse and I become angry and frustrated, the memories I maintain of that disagreement remain and still contain the anger. When I am happy, the memory of that argument will fade, but the next time I become angry again, the memory of the previous arguments will come to mind and reinforce my anger. This explains why we become so negative and focused on all the faults of our spouses when we are angry. We accumulate all the anger and frustration of all the times we have fought.

The same is true in the opposite sense, and some scientists believe that this causes the sensation of love. When John first meets Mary, an attractive girl, and she shows him attention, this generates a strong positive emotion in John linked to the idea of Mary. As their relationship continues and she smiles at his anecdotes, laughs at his jokes, and gazes into his eyes, he continues to connect happiness with Mary. As they begin getting physical—kissing, hugging, and finally having sex—this happiness for John has now reached ecstasy, and that is strongly linked to the image and name of Mary. Thus, he only has to think of Mary and he feels happy and ecstatic and has butterflies in his stomach. Every time he is happy, the image of Mary comes to mind. He is in love! Think back to your courtship. Didn't something similar happen to you?

What happens then? John marries Mary and now when he talks, she snaps at him. When he tells jokes, she ignores him. And finally when he makes sexual advances, she rejects him. He now links many negative behaviors that he had not previously seen to his image of Mary. This is the end of the fantasy stage and the beginning of reality. In part, it happens to everyone, but if we start focusing only on the negatives, and there is little positive remaining, the love slowly dies. Every time John now thinks of Mary, anger and frustration come to mind. Every time he is angry or hurt, the image of Mary appears. The positive emotion that Mary generated in him has disappeared and John feels miserable with Mary. Be assured that the same has happened to Mary too.

There have to be more positive than negative emotions linked to our mate in our brain, or state dependent memory will associate that person only to the negative qualities.

The good thing about this is that we can control this emotional experience according to what we focus on. As a result, people who focus on the positive in their lives and in their relationships are more satisfied and enjoy life and their companion more. They may have just as many trials and difficulties in life and just as many conflicts in their relationship, but they have the power to search for the positive and reinforce these memories and experiences in their brain. We create our own happiness!

It is not possible to provide positive reassurances to each other if we only focus on the negative. We have to open our eyes and our minds to what we like, admire, and respect in our spouse and keep it in our daily awareness and express it. Some people become so overwhelmed with the negatives that they are no longer able to see what is right and wonderful about their spouse. What makes the difference? There may be many reasons, but one is fundamental—not bearing grudges. Another word for this is forgiveness—forgiveness of the small slights and misunderstandings that occur in every relationship.

Why does this seem so difficult? Several factors interfere with our correct perception of the action of others. If you were to see a young lady come into a meeting, stumble on the carpet, drop her briefcase with all the papers dropping out, and lose her glasses in the process, what would be your opinion of her? If later she also spills her coffee, you would probably judge her to be clumsy. Would you take into consideration other external reasons that might have made her trip? New shoes, old prescription glasses, or just nervousness for the meeting could all explain her behavior. Maybe she tripped because she was on a plane all night and is now exhausted and has swollen feet. The tendency that we all have to judge other people's negative actions in terms of internal, rather than external causes, is called Fundamental Attribution Effect. When others, including our spouse, do something negative, we conclude it is because that is the way they are—it is part of their character, and therefore there is little possibility to change it. This colors all our perceptions of other people's actions.

Of course, we are far gentler with ourselves. We are aware of all the external circumstances that affect our behavior, and so we tend to justify ourselves according to what happens to us. Rarely do we have the same tolerance for others. Therefore, we justify ourselves. If you handed in a report and received it back from your supervisor with the comment, "Well done, I've never seen a better analysis," you will tend to explain this according to your internal disposition—I worked hard and used my intelligence and communication skills to produce a great analysis. If instead the report came back with a comment like, "Very inadequate, the worst I have seen in months," chances are you would explain this by external factors like: I didn't have enough time or my supervisor didn't give me any indication what he was looking for. We explain our successes with our internal character, but we excuse our failures by citing external situational events. The opposite is often true in how we judge other people's work.

These biases are so much a part of us that we often do not even notice them, but they can be detrimental in a relationship. When we snap at our spouse, it is because we had a bad day and are tired. But if he snaps, it is because he is insensitive. That is, we ascribe the cause of our behavior to external events (bad day) and that of our spouse to internal characteristics (insensitive). When this happens repeatedly, we confirm our belief that it is just the way he is, and we convince ourselves that we have married an insensitive brute, or a wife with constant mood swings. It may be another month or more before our spouse snaps again, but now each time he does, it confirms our opinion that that is the way he is. Since it is part of their history, it is unchangeable, and we wonder how we could have married such a brute.

We focus our attention on the negative, and in the end, that is all we see. We do not see the dozens of occasions when our spouse is kind, generous, or loving; we see only the irritable or grumpy behavior. This is compounded by the fact that you can't see and therefore don't notice "non-behavior." That is, we don't know how many times our spouse wanted to say something nasty and refrained because of courtesy, respect, or convenience. We do not see the self-restraint; we only see the behavior. We reinforce this with our language by using words like *always* and *never*. So the conversation often becomes something like, "Why are you *always* so angry?" How can the other person defend himself? Can he or she cite all the times that they were not angry, or angry but said nothing? It becomes an illogical conversation because there is no defense, just perceptions.

How can we move beyond this and perceive the positive? One way is training.

Good humor isn't a trait of character, it is an art that requires practice.[4]
—David Seabury

We generally have little training in seeing things positively. Maybe because our parents criticized us more than they praised us, we tend to see this as natural. If I ask a class of students to express the positive and negative aspects of a speech or interview performed by a classmate, they will immediately bring up all the mistakes that the student made, but they have a hard time seeing or talking about the positive aspects. We tend to focus on the negative, and it takes effort to avoid this. The same is true of our spouse and our relationship.

A second aspect may be one of humility.

Without humility there can be no humanity.[5]

—John Buchan

Judge not, that ye be not judged.

—Matthew 7:1

Humility means recognizing that just as our spouse has defects, annoying behaviors, and immature attitudes, so do we. Just as I have to put up with my spouse, she has to put up with me. Somehow, we lose this idea, probably because of the self-serving bias mentioned above. We tend to protect our egos and see ourselves as being better than we really are. We over-emphasize the good qualities and believe that they are internal and part of us and under-emphasize the bad, blaming them on external events. We rarely have the same clemency for our spouse. We should listen more to our soul in those rare moments of self-clarity and realize that our spouse shows similar forbearance with our defects. A good question to ask yourself frequently is, "How would it be to be married to me?" We should be grateful when our spouse has been particularly patient with us during a bad day or bad period. In fact, we should express that gratitude and sincerely thank them for what they do for us. When was the last time that you expressed thanks to your wife or husband?

Finally, it is necessary that we learn to forgive. We all make mistakes, and if there is no tolerance for the errors of our spouse, the relationship cannot endure. There may be a limit beyond which we cannot continue tolerating our spouse's behavior, particularly if it destroys all trust, but there must be an ample margin for errors along the way. The concept of the relationship is that of growth. No one begins the journey already perfect, mature, or even close to being so. The important idea is that we can see beyond the mistakes of today to the potential of tomorrow.

> *Wherefore, I say unto you, that ye ought to forgive one another; for he that forgiveth not his brother his trespasses standeth condemned before the Lord; for these remaineth in him the greater sin.*
> —Doctrine and Covenants 64:9

> *The weak can never forgive. Forgiveness is the attribute of the strong.*[6]
> —Mahatma Gandhi

> *I can forgive, but I cannot forget, is only another way of saying, I will not forgive. Forgiveness ought to be like a cancelled note—torn in two, and burned up, so that it never can be shown against one.*[7]
> —Henry Ward Beecher

A story written by Larry Hiller published in the *New Era* magazine in 1985 has remained with me for many years. It is the story of a certain Malcolm Trent, and we can summarize it as follows:

Malcolm was a young man when he began putting pebbles in his pockets. The first time was when his supervisor, Mr. Grump, got mad at him for something he had not done. He couldn't defend himself or say what he thought to Mr. Grump for fear of being fired, and he had no one he could share his anger with, but within himself he said, "I have to do something to remember this so I will never forget it." He still had the same thought that evening as he was waiting for the bus home, and seeing a pebble on the sidewalk in front of him, he suddenly had an idea.

"I will pick up this pebble and stick it in my pocket, and every time I feel it there, I can remember what happened," Malcolm told himself.

That evening he put the pebble with his keys and wallet, and then the next day put it back in his trousers' pocket, where he would touch it and feel all his anger all over again. It seemed that Mr. Grump had forgotten the entire affair, but not Malcolm—no way!

This worked so well that the next evening when a taxi did not stop to pick him up in the pouring rain, he found another stone to remember that slight too. Then there was one for the salesclerk who did not give him the correct change, another for the newspaper boy who sent his newspaper into a puddle, and one for his neighbor whose dog disturbed him with his barking. As time went on, he found that all sorts of people and situations irritated him.

He also found one day in the grocery store, to his embarrassment, that with his pockets full of stones and pebbles, his belt was not sufficient to keep his pants up. Therefore, he ordered some extra strong suspenders. Then, his pant pockets just could not hold any more rocks, so he bought a jacket with many pockets.

After time, even this was not enough. He would walk around, and all his pockets would bulge with stones, gravel, and pebbles. His clothes always had an odor of dust and grime, and everything sagged with the weight of the rocks. Most people would just give up but not Malcolm. He was afraid that he would forget the mean things that others had done to him. Maybe they did not intend to irritate him, and maybe they were not even aware of what they had done, but he would not forget! He bought a large briefcase so that he could always keep it near him and stored more rocks and pebbles there.

As the years passed, his collection of stones spilled over to the rooms of his house. His closets were full of rocks, as were his bathtub, furniture, and floors. There were piles everywhere. Sometimes he would put some rocks in his bed, just to remind himself how hateful some people had been. His neighbors, coworkers, and family gradually avoided him because he became more withdrawn and suspicious. Every day he became more like his rocks—hard, cold, rough, and gray.

He might have passed his days immersed in his rocks, reliving the hurtful memories if one day Professor Igneous had not called. Dr. Igneous was a famous geologist from the nearby university and had heard of

Malcolm's collection of rocks. He asked if he could bring some students with him and come and visit the collection. Malcolm, hesitant, made an appointment for the following Saturday. Malcolm was excited and nervous for this visit and spent his time trying to polish and wash his stones, but there were just too many.

Finally the day came and Professor Igneous arrived with seven of his best pupils. Several had mining tools, rock hammers, and magnifying glasses. Expecting a collection of precious gems and crystals, they remained stunned and bewildered when they entered Malcolm's home and had to push their way through piles of common rock, gravel, pebbles, and stones. There were even pieces of concrete and asphalt. Malcolm, who was expecting a reaction of awe and admiration, was disconcerted by the silence that settled on the group.

Professor Igneous, who was a kind, understanding man, seeing Malcolm's nervousness, acted as though nothing was out of place and complemented Malcolm on his collection. He then took a stone from a pile and asked him, "Maybe, Mr. Trent, you could tell us why you started your collection and why you saved this particular rock?" Malcolm was extremely nervous, started swallowing quickly, and realized that it had been years since he had sat down and had a normal conversation with someone.

He explained, "Each rock represents a time when someone slighted me or made me sad or angry. These rocks are in memory of those sad events."

He looked at the stone in the professor's hand and said hesitantly, "That particular rock was when the dry cleaners didn't deliver my shirts on time. Or maybe, maybe it was when my favorite TV series was canceled. Or was it when someone dialed a wrong number?" Malcolm realized with horror that he did not really remember.

The professor, seeing Malcolm's uneasiness, said, "Thank you very much to have invited us into your home and to have shown us this rock collection. I believe that it is unique. Before we leave, could you show us your other collection?"

"Other collection?" Malcolm asked. "I don't have any other collection."

"You don't?" asked Dr. Igneous. "I would have thought that you would have another collection for all the times that someone was nice to you or did you a favor or just smiled at you."

"No," Malcolm explained. "This is my only collection."

"Could you tell us then, Mr. Trent," Dr. Igneous asked, "do any of your neighbors have a similar collection for all the times that you grumbled or slighted them? Maybe we could go visit their collection."

Again, Malcolm had to reply, "No, I don't know of anyone else who has a similar collection."

"Well then, thank you for your time," said the professor as he filed out with his students.

Malcolm was left alone with his rocks, but somehow they did not satisfy him anymore. They were cold, gray, dusty, and dirty. The words of the professor echoed in his mind, while he was surrounded with the silence of the rocks. He spent days just sitting there, almost petrified, immobile as a stone, until he realized—*I have become just like my rocks.*

He decided that he needed to get rid of his collection, so he put up a sign saying, "Rocks, gravel, and pebbles free." No one came; no one was interested. He then tried hiring a maid, requesting that she clean up the house and get rid of the rocks, but in the face of such a daunting task, no one would accept the job. Finally, he realized that only he could eliminate his rocks and his memories, so he hired a dump truck. For days, dust surrounded his house as he kept shoveling rocks into the truck until not one was left in his house.

Now as he goes to work, his neighbors greet him, and his coworkers compliment him on his sharp-looking clothes. His house is clean and resplendent, and his garden is full of shrubs, trees, and flowers. None of his neighbors know what gave him such a sudden interest in his garden, but his next-door-neighbor, Mrs. Kratz, noticed that after she had brought him a slice of cake one day, he went out in the garden and planted another flower.[8]

Are you picking up and hoarding stones so that you can remember every mistake your spouse has ever made, or are you planting flowers? Try this one exercise; it can improve your marriage immensely. Each day, look for and find at least one thing for which you can compliment your spouse. Then express it to him or her. Notice the way they dress, the small attentions they pay you, or the routine things that they take care of that you now take for granted. Notice and express your gratitude. When you start searching for the positive, the mind will seek it and find it. That is what you will focus on.

The compliment should not be generic or the same each day. Telling your wife, "Oh, good meal tonight," does not say much. If you repeat it often, it may even make her feel that you just say it to say it. Be specific. Say, "I like the way you are always able to create a well-balanced meal and also make it so tasty." Alternatively, "I like the way you smile and your whole face lights up; it makes me feel warm inside."

Seek out the positive. Focus your attention on what your spouse does for you, the differences that make you grow, the small acts of kindness, the simple fact that they are the person they are.

For where your treasure is, there will your heart be also.
—Matthew 6:21

Is your mate your treasure? One reason that this seems so difficult to do is that we have little experience with positive emotions. We all have past experiences of disappointment or disillusionment. Children have little awareness or understanding, so punishments or disappointments seem to come unexpectedly to them with no forewarning and are very threatening. Therefore, they start anticipating that bad things will happen, maybe unexpectedly, and are afraid to feel too good for fear that it will not last. The Hendricks validate this concept in their book *Conscious Loving*:

> We all know how to feel bad, and we know how to feel neutral. What we need to learn is how to feel good . . . . We are programmed that we cannot feel good for very long without invoking some negative experience to bring us down.[9]

We are afraid to feel good. For years my motto, as a true pessimist, was "Blessed is he who expects the worse, for he will not be disappointed." Many people have a limit to how good they can allow themselves to feel and will purposely, albeit unconsciously, do something to end feeling happy. Some people worry over possible futures just to keep themselves down. Others will pick an argument just when everything is going so well. Others will bury their feelings with alcohol, drugs, overeating, or other compulsive behaviors.

Still another study has found that the major difference between satisfied and dissatisfied couples is that the happier couples have a better sense of humor. The ability to laugh at ourselves and to laugh at what happens around us is not only a stress reliever, but it means that we are viewing life and our relationship in a positive way. When was the last time you laughed together? Living together should be joyful. There should be fun, not just duties and responsibilities. If you are too overwhelmed in diapers, career expectations, or routine, it is time to find the fun of being together. Start thinking, "How could I make our relationship more fun?" Make a list of fun things to do together.

FUN THINGS

Things we can do together to enjoy life and each other more:

1.

2.

3.

4.

5.

It is not just in your relationship that you need to seek the positive but in your whole life. You need to count your blessings. Look around you and start appreciating what you have in life, not what you do not have. Start looking at what your mate does for you, not what she does not do. Get involved with people less fortunate than you. Seek the positive in life, and life will become joyful.

Another suggestion is to keep a gratitude journal. Start writing down all the good things that happen to you—for example, all the beautiful experiences and sunsets you see—and write all the things you are grateful for about your mate. Keep this diary daily and read it often, and you cannot help but focus on the good things. When you are feeling neglected by your spouse, just go back to your diary and find the many things that he or she has done for you. Not only will this increase your appreciation of your spouse, but it will also help you to count your blessings and be grateful to God for your life and make you happier.

Remember too the magic number five. Remember every day to make sure that you have given at least five positive messages for any possible negative slight that might have occurred.

If you only see the weeds and dead leaves in your garden, you will never enjoy the beauty of the flowers.

NOTES
1. Michael Michalko, *Thinkertoys* (Berkeley: Ten Speed Press, 1991), 161.
2. *Quotationary* (NovaSoft, 1999).
3. John Gottman, PhD, *Why Marriages Succeed or Fail* (New York: Fireside, 1995).
4. *Quotationary* (NovaSoft, 1999).
5. *Quotationary* (NovaSoft, 1999).

6. Mahatma Gandhi. Quoted on *The Quotation Page*; available from www.quotation-spage.com.

7. Henry Ward Beecher. Quoted in *Think Exist*; available from www.en.thinkexist.com/quotation.

8. Larry A. Hiller, "Pockets Full of Rocks," *New Era*, Mar. 1985.

9. Gay and Kathlyn Hendricks, PhDs, *Conscious Loving: The Journey to Co-Commitment* (New York: Bantam Books, 1992).

Rule 7

CREATIVELY SOLVE THE CONFLICT

And if thy brother or sister offend thee, thou shalt take him or her between him or her and three alone; and if he or she confess thou shalt be reconciled.

—Doctrine and Covenants 42:88

Dave: Oh, by the way, my mother is coming to see us for the holidays. Is that okay with you?

Jane: And when did you two decide this? I don't remember you calling her recently.

Dave: Oh, she just happened to call last week, and we thought it would be good for the kids to see their grandmother at Christmas. They see so little of her.

Jane: Oh, you decided that together, did you? And you thought you would pop it on me now. I guess you were waiting for the right moment to communicate your decision. You always make the decision anyway, so why ask me?

Dave: You see, you are always so sarcastic. I was asking you. Didn't you hear me ask a question?

Jane: So now I'm sarcastic. And what are you—Mr. Perfect? I suppose that when you forgot to pick up Joey from school to take him to the dental appointment, you were showing your perfection?

Dave: What does Joey's dental appointment have to do with anything? You are so irrational. There is never a right moment with you. You are on permanent PMS.

Jane: Oh great. I suppose by offending me you can hide what you are really doing. Well, if you really loved me, you would have more respect. Can't you see what you are doing? You would do anything possible to avoid your family. Christmas is the only time we have together as a family. You never spend time with me or the kids, and now this.

Dave: So what am I suppose to do, call my mother and tell her that you don't want her seeing the kids? You never could stand that I have a better relation with my mom than you have with your family. Admit it!

Jane: Oh, do whatever you want; that's what you do anyway. How could I expect that this time would be any different?

Does this sound familiar? Did Dave and Jane solve anything? Can you think back to arguments you have had that were just as bitter and in which you never really solved anything? Why does there have to be conflict? What causes it, and how can it be resolved? These are some of the questions that we need to answer in this chapter.

We made the statement in an earlier chapter that where there are differences, there will always be conflict. We have also affirmed that everyone is different and that there are fundamental differences between the sexes so that this conflict is assured. We have also implied that this conflict is positive if it is resolved in a creative and positive way. Some marriage manuals concentrate almost exclusively on communication and conflict management, and this is certainly an important aspect of a happy marriage. I believe, however, that if we give more emphasis to the positive behaviors of proactive love, service, trust, and commitment, with realistic expectations, many of the problems of conflict and communication will not exist.

If we are convinced of our spouse's good faith, that he or she would not knowingly hurt us—if we have trust—we are less likely to misinterpret their statements in a negative way, and we are more open to other possible explanations. If we have realistic expectations, we are less likely to expect our spouse to read our minds or to understand our needs so we will be more direct in our communications. In addition, if we have a better understanding of how the opposite sex solves problems and communicates and we value those differences, we are more tolerant of those differences. Given this, however, even the most loving couples will have conflict and can hurt each other, so it is important to understand why conflict occurs and find some creative ways of solving the differences.

WHY CONFLICT OCCURS

The first reason for conflict, and the most common, is a difference in opinion, belief, need, or value. When two people have different opinions, they have several options. Let us say that Jane wants to go out for the evening with her husband, Kevin, but he is tired and doesn't want to. Jane can say, "Okay, I will stay at home with you." On the other hand, she can convince Kevin to go out with her, but he probably will do so against his will. Or, she can go out and he can stay at home, but they will not be together. Finally, one or the other gives in, but there is the implicit or explicit agreement that next time the other one decides. None of these solutions totally satisfies either person, but this is part of the give and take of a relationship and does not have to lead to conflict. This simple example, though, can mask differences in personality or needs. Kevin has a physically demanding job and is truly tired. Jane has been at home with the kids all day and is climbing the walls. Or maybe Kevin is an introvert and hates social affairs, where he feels out of place and overwhelmed, or Jane is an extrovert and needs stimulus otherwise she becomes bored and bitter. Now, if Jane *always* has to give in and the couple *never* gets out, or if Kevin feels violated because Jane is *always* dragging him around, then conflict arises. When the contrast is not just about frivolous activities or superficial opinions but is about something that is actually important to one or the other or both, negotiating a compromise rarely satisfies either person. For example, if I want to bring up my children in a religious faith and my spouse does not, to say, "I'll bring up the first child with religion and you can bring up the next one without religion," wouldn't satisfy either one of us.

Much of the ongoing conflict in a relationship has to do with our expectation of what is the right and the wrong way to do things. This can be over things as banal as when to pay the bills or clean the dishes or as important as to how to educate the children or deal with family members. We have a belief that is often unconscious of what is the correct way of doing something and that any other way is wrong.

One of the reasons for this is that our parents and school teachers trained us to think that there is just one right way to do things. When my mate sees things or does things differently, then it is necessarily the wrong way. We name this tendency to analyze a problem from just one perspective convergent thinking.

Given that most of us are logical creatures, the way we think about the world and solve our daily problems uses some form of analysis. That is, we tend to take a large problem and start breaking it down into smaller pieces until we come up with the right answer. From our parents we learned that there is a right way (their way) and a wrong way to do just about anything. Teachers have reinforced this by rewarding the right answer and discouraging the wrong answer. It is estimated that by the time a student finishes college, he will have taken more than 2,600 exams and quizzes. In all of these, he must give the right answer to each question. Can you remember ever taking a test that asked for many right answers? Our grades most of the time depend on how many right answers we give. We then start with a variety of choices and narrow them down and finally converge our thinking to come up with the right answer—and every other answer is wrong. A diagram of this is the following:

When we leave the realm of school and logic and enter human affairs, rarely does this type of thinking work well, and no one has trained us in any other way of thinking. Thus, one partner's perception of the world sees the problem, breaks it down, and comes up with a "right" answer. The other spouse, with different perceptions, sees the problem, breaks it down logically,

Problem

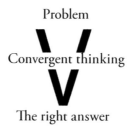

Convergent thinking

The right answer

and comes up with a different "right" answer. The couple may then argue, even for years, not over which answer is more functional for them but over who is right and who is wrong. Most people who go to marital therapy are not looking for a different take on their problem but for a judge who will decide who is right and who is wrong. Dr. Phil said the following:

> We make ourselves right, because that's what we treasure in life, being right. . . . Seldom did either spouse in the marriage come to me and say, "Dr. McGraw, I want our marriage to work, no matter who is right." What both of them said, in effect was, "I want you to recognize that I am right, and convince my spouse that I am right, so that we can do things my way."[1]

As long as each person in the couple thinks in terms of what is right and what is wrong, conflict will continue. Both are frozen into rigid patterns of thinking and rarely can entertain other options. Think back on the last major argument you had with your spouse. Did you solve it? Do you still believe that you are right and he or she is wrong? Why?

The more fundamental question is: is there ever a right or wrong answer? Is any one solution to a problem absolutely the correct one that will be correct forever? The more people become aware of other cultures and other ways of thinking, the less absolute any solution is. If we are two separate individuals who have created our own unique relationship, then the solutions of our parents, friends, or even the psychologists on TV or in books will not necessarily be the perfect or right answers. These are answers that each couple has to search for.

If we look at the above argument between Jane and Dave, we find that each is influenced by several assumptions that they believe are right. For Dave, it is right that his mother can visit and interact with her grandchildren. Who can argue with that? Jane in fact doesn't argue that but argues that it is good and necessary that the family have more quality time together, particularly with their father, and that Christmas is the best time for this. That is right too, and obviously, Grandmother will interfere. So, who is right? Is there any absolute right answer to this dilemma? No. The couple will have to work out an alternative answer that satisfies both Dave and Jane. What this case illustrates is a difference in needs and who can say which need is greater or more important.

The problem with the above argument is that Dave and Jane are not discussing their different needs rationally and coming to some logical conclusion. Conflict and arguments are rarely rational and usually involve anger, frustration, and misunderstandings. Conflict is emotional and involves almost all the negative emotions. We come away from the fight feeling misunderstood, unloved, and hurt. This is the second reason for conflict—misunderstanding and emotional baggage. Almost all marriage manuals give advice on how to make fights more logical, but I have found that it rarely works because the essence of the conflict is about the emotional hurt, and this almost always comes from our past.

As we have already discussed, most negative emotions are triggered by a perception of threat. Our bodies are programmed to react automatically whenever we are faced with danger. If you see a snake in the room with you, before you can logically analyze the event, your body is already reacting by increasing your heart rate, breathing, tensing your muscles, and so on. We call this the fright-flight-fight response. These physiological reactions are also linked to emotions, and in the case of the snake, we would call that emotion fear. The important thing is that the reaction is automatic and unconscious. It will be the same whether it is a harmless garden snake or a deadly rattler as long as we perceive it as dangerous. Our brain stores information about all the past experiences of perceived danger, both physical and psychological danger, so that it can react immediately to the threat. We then react physically and emotionally to any situation similar to the original threatening experience. Just like the garden snake, however, it is not the actual threat that triggers this but our perception that there is a threat. How did we form these perceptions?

The biggest cause of our emotional baggage is our own history of insecurities and past traumas. These cloud our perceptions and expectations to the point where we see threats and danger when there are none. For example, Jane from the above example maybe has a strong sense of abandonment and rejection because her parents divorced when she was young and deep inside she suffered from her father leaving the family. She is now going to be particularly sensitive to any sign that Dave is giving priority to his work or is emotionally closer to his mother than to her. She may be reacting to a situation that does not exist at all. Dave loves her, but her past intrudes and makes her insecure, and she overreacts. Dave, on the other hand, came from a family in which his father heavily criticized him. He has learned to attack whenever he feels that someone, in this case Jane, does not agree with him, and may be criticizing him. He then overreacts and attacks.

The more unresolved emotional baggage we have, the more frequently we will misperceive a situation and overreact. Therefore, the more frequent the fights, the more emotionally intense they will be. As time goes on, we create emotional baggage from the relationship itself. Things that our spouse has done or said in the past become part of our perceptions of who they are and what their intentions are. We create memories of past situations in which we felt threatened and hurt by our spouse, and these become new triggers for similar situations. We could suppose that in Jane's case, there are a series of negative experiences with Dave and his mother in which she felt threatened, creating an automatic trigger even when there may be no threat.

What is sad is that most couples do not realize what has happened and therefore argue about trivial details rather than the real issue. This focus on seemingly irrelevant details is called a ghost conflict. When I was growing up in the sixties, there was an episode that made the national news about a man who requested a divorce because his wife squeezed the toothpaste tube from the middle, and he just couldn't stand it anymore. Unless he was a pathological neat freak, this was probably a ghost conflict, and the real problem was some underlying conflict symbolized by the behavior. One can imagine that the real conflict in this case was really about orderliness, or cleanliness, and probably several unrealistic expectations were involved. How often have you argued over small things that do not really matter? Why? Did you ever solve the issue?

Before we discuss the principles of how to creatively solve conflict, it might be worthwhile to examine common approaches to conflict that most of us use.

COMMON APPROACHES TO CONFLICT

Because most of us do not like conflict and we feel threatened by the anger and frustration that accompanies it, we each have a different pattern of behavior to deal with it. The most common strategy is avoidance. This strategy seems more common in men than in women, particularly in relationships. The ostrich sticks his head in the sand and pretends that there is no problem. Actually, there are several different reasons and strategies used by avoiders. Some avoid the conflict because they are fearful of the result. They are afraid that if they confront the other person, they will damage the relationship. Others avoid because they do not believe that there is a solution to the problem. The more we perceive that the problem is caused by inherent, internal, long-lasting characteristics of our spouse that can't be changed, the more of this type of avoidance there will be. Many sidestep conflict by creating diversions or by arguing over ghost conflicts rather than confronting the real issue.

At times there are no solutions to conflict, and sometimes problems do go away by themselves. But usually the result of sticking one's head in the sand is that the problem becomes more severe and urgent. Not only that, but the other spouse can become frustrated, and misconceptions can remain and worsen. Like any strategy that does not allow confrontation in the end, we deny ourselves the benefits of clarifying the conflict and seeing things from another perspective.

When we were first married, my wife, Fernanda, would begin an argument with an emotional outburst. As soon as I heard her anger, I would immediately close up, not say a word, and sit there, listening and cringing. She would get so frustrated that she would yell at me, "Say something!" I thought I was doing the right thing by controlling myself, but in the end, I only wanted to avoid the emotions that were too uncomfortable for me. I do not know if she appreciates the change, but I definitely participate in discussions today!

The Lord has advised against avoidance:

> And if thy brother or sister offend thee, thou shalt take him or her between him or her and thee alone; and if he or she confess thou shalt be reconciled. (Doctrine and Covenants 42:88)

This tells us that we should confront the person whom we believe has offended us and seek reconciliation. It also instructs us that this is a private matter. One of the worst things that a couple can do is involve other family members or friends in their arguments. This does not build trust; but rather, it is a subtle form of betrayal. This is your soul mate. An argument is a means to better understanding your spouse's point of view and expressing yours. It is an opportunity to draw closer and touch each other's minds and souls if done correctly, so do not avoid it!

Another strategy is the conquest approach. The conqueror wants to win, to be right, and to prove his or her spouse wrong. He, and it often is a he, needs to score a victory. Our society so deeply ingrains the concept of competition, of winning and achieving a goal at all costs, that many people are not able to separate the competition in the work place, which is bad enough, from competition at home and in the marriage. The spouse that has to be right will try to win every conflict by overpowering his spouse. Each spouse uses the power that they have whether verbal, emotional, economic, authoritative or, unfortunately, physical. Domestic abuse is the number one cause of death in women under forty in the United States. The downside of the conquest method is that for someone to win there has to be a loser. This approach polarizes the position of the antagonists and reduces the possibility for negotiations. In addition, the person with the most power in the relationship will usually win, which perpetuates an unbalanced and unhealthy rapport. This cannot be the approach used in a loving relationship because very quickly, trust is betrayed and the relationship will shrivel.

There are other approaches to conflict that are subtler but also have negative consequences. The most common is bargaining or compromise. Many manuals advise to use some type of bargaining or negotiations in which I give up something and you give up something too so that we can meet in some middle ground. Although this may be part of getting along in which we forfeit some things that are less important to us for the good of the relationship, too often it can lead to a lose-lose approach to conflict resolution in which neither spouse is happy with the solution. This approach also defines power as what we can get the other person to give up, so it becomes a milder form of conquest. Who can judge the value of one person's goals or needs compared to the others? What may seem like a small request to us may be a great sacrifice for our spouse. With this approach, we are keeping some type of tally in our head as to who has given what in the past, which may be okay in business but not in love.

A final approach used often is the band-aid or quick-fix method. We come up with an immediate answer to the problem but never face the real disagreement. We may work out an agreement about whom we will visit for Christmas, but we have not faced the problems of our relationship with the in-laws and with each other. Much like the avoidance approach, we never face the issues, and the problem often grows worse and the misperceptions increase. In addition, the band-aid approach gives the false illusion that something has been done about the conflict, when in fact nothing has changed.

The problem with approaching conflict using any of these methods is that as soon as people feel threatened or frustrated by their spouse, they go on the defensive and start using one or more of the following defense mechanisms. Try to see how many are your personal favorites.

DIRTY FIGHTING TECHNIQUES

(Modified from Family Advocacy Domestic Violence Prevention Program[2])

Indicate how frequently you use each of the following techniques when you fight with your spouse using the following criteria:

0 Never
1 Rarely
2 Sometimes
3 Often

_____ 1. *Blaming*—Make it clear that any fault lies entirely with your spouse and that you are simply the innocent victim. Do not admit that your behavior has anything to do with the problem, and make sure your spouse knows that you will never give in or change first.

_____ 2. *Over generalizing*—Make sure to use words like *never* and *always* in phrases like "You *always* pay more attention to others and *never* pay attention to me." This will probably distract your spouse enough to argue about the generalization rather then face the real problem.

_____ 3. *Timing*—Pick the right time to begin an argument, preferably late at night when you are both tired, or during your spouse's favorite TV show or activity. As a rule, pick a time that they least expect it and are least able to respond.

_____ 4. *Escalating*—Move quickly from the issue to questioning your spouse's personality, to wondering whether it is worth staying together, following this structure: issue—personality—relationship. Use your spouse's shortcomings as evidence of bad faith and the impossibility of ever having a happy relationship.

_____ 5. *Kitchen sinking*—Never stick to the original issue but throw in as many problems in detail as possible. Do not limit yourself to the present but dredge up as much of the past as possible. If your spouse cannot remember it, that is his or her problem.

_____ 6. *Labeling*—By labeling somebody in a negative way, you create the impression that your spouse is totally at fault. Psychological labels such as immature, neurotic, or paranoid are particularly useful to obscure areas in which you may feel vulnerable.

_____ 7. *Cross complaining*—Respond to any complaint that your spouse makes with one of your own. For example, "Me, late? Well, if it weren't for the fact that you never iron my shirts, then I wouldn't be late." If used properly, you can counter balance complaints indefinitely.

_____ 8. *Asking Why*—"Why didn't you clean the kitchen?" or "Why are you late?" These questions imply that there is something terribly wrong with your spouse and there is a far more severe issue than whatever you were discussing.

_____ 9. *Listing Injustices*—This is a great morale builder. By reciting every slight, injustice, or inequity you have ever suffered in the relationship, you will experience a renewed sense of self-righteousness. You can use this to justify just about any behavior you want. For example, "Since you bought that dress, I can buy a new car."

_____ 10. *Mind Reading*—By deciding that you know the real reason that your spouse is acting that way, you can avoid having to debate issues. For example, "You don't really feel that way." Also, "You only say that to appease me," is particularly effective.

_____ 11. *Fortune Telling*—Predicting the future can save you the effort of really trying to resolve the problem. "You will never change" or

"It would be easy for me to change, but you would never live up to it" are statements that can protect you from having to make a change.

_____ 12. *Being Sarcastic*—This is a great way of clearly implying something without having to take responsibility for it. If you say, "You're so smart," in just the right way, you can imply that they are stupid and deny that you said it at the same time.

_____ 13. *Avoiding Responsibility*—Although saying, "I can't remember," is not a particularly elegant method, it can be quite effective. Using alcohol or fatigue can work too. "I must have been drunk."

_____ 14. *Playing the Martyr*—If timed properly, this tactic can completely disorient the opposition. "You're right, dear, I am hopeless" can stop your spouse cold. A less subtle form is, "How could you do that after all I have done for you?"

_____ 15. *Give Advice*—By telling people how they should act, think, or behave, particularly done in a cold, rational voice, can give you a position of superiority while insisting that you are only trying to be helpful.

_____ 16. *Use Relatives*—"When you do that you are just like your mother." Alternatively, "You're going to end up an alcoholic and a loser just like your father" can undermine confidence and deviate the discussion, besides making stabs at family members you do not like.

_____ 17. *Being Inconsistent*—Keep your spouse off balance by frequently changing positions. Try complaining that your spouse never talks to you, and then ignore anything he or she may have to say.

_____ 18. *Reject Compromise*—Do not back down. Why settle for compromise when with a little luck you can really devastate your spouse (and destroy the relationship)? Stick with the "one winner" approach.

_____ 19. *Leave*—When all else fails, walk out. No problem is so big or important that you cannot ignore it. Walk out of the room or the house or just refuse to talk. If you are too lazy to leave, maybe you can get away with just the threat to leave.

_____ 20. *Other*—This is your chance to be creative. Use the children, money, dominating, pulling rank, or any of your favorite improvisations.

List at least two dirty fighting techniques that *you* use that create misunderstandings and escalate conflict.

What can you do to eliminate these?

CREATIVE CONFLICT MANAGEMENT

Although the above list of techniques may be humorous when we read them in a book, they can be deadly in a relationship. They have no place in a celestial marriage. There is no excuse for soul mates calling each other names, using sarcasm, criticizing, blaming, labeling, or making comparisons to undesired relatives. Does this sound as if you are loving, honoring, or cherishing your spouse? Can this build trust or commitment? You should never purposely hurt your spouse! This list is there so that you can recognize how you defend yourself and resolve not to do it anymore.

The Lord is clear on how we should regulate our relationship, and he particularly addresses this to the priesthood. Doctrine and Covenants 121:39–42 is one of my favorite scriptures because it is a complete marriage manual wrapped up in just a few verses:

> We have learned by sad experience that it is the nature and disposition of almost all men, as soon as they get a little authority, as they suppose, they will immediately begin to exercise unrighteous dominion. Hence many are called, but few are chosen. No power or influence can or ought to be maintained by virtue of the priesthood, only by persuasion, by long-suffering, by gentleness and meekness, and by love unfeigned. By kindness and pure knowledge, which shall greatly enlarge the soul without hypocrisy, and without guile.

Do you find anger, criticism, or sarcasm anywhere in these words? How then can we solve our conflicts? What do we do when our mate hurts us, willingly or not? This is where the "work" of relationships comes to play. The work is overcoming our weaknesses, controlling our anger, and working in the context of the gospel to find a solution.

We have stated that conflict will occur in any relationship because people are different, because they have unmet needs, and because misunderstandings can happen. How then can we resolve these without damaging the relationship? Some arguments are over minor issues. Help clear the air. We must learn what is important to our spouse that we were not necessarily aware of before. When more important issues are involved, however, it can be helpful to work through the steps of creative conflict resolution to find better solutions to our problems. This will be particularly effective for ongoing conflict that reoccurs regularly or that causes a lot of resentment.

There are some principles that have to regulate conflict resolutions if we want to use our differences to build a better relationship rather than destroy what we have. The first principle is that this must be "we," not "me against you." *We* are working *together* to better *our* relationship. There can be no competition and no I-win- you-lose attitudes, or the relationship will suffer. Some people call this the conflict partnership. Resolution has to occur within the context of the relationship. A second principle is that the confrontation's goal is to improve the relationship. For example, avoiding a conflict means that we prefer the status quo rather than growing and improving the rapport that we have. As a consequence of these two principles, any solution must have mutual benefits; it must be win-win. Each person learns more about the other and becomes more aware of the other person's needs and potential positive power.

There are five steps to conflict resolution:

1. Examine our perceptions and expectations; search for alternative answers.
2. Examine our needs, our spouse's needs, and the relationship needs.
3. Confront.
4. Search for solutions.
5. Implement and evaluate.

The first step to solving a problem is to identify what the real conflict is. This sounds so easy, but it is often the most difficult part. What is the real issue? Why am I, or why is my spouse, so angry? How many times have we begun complaining or criticizing something in our spouse to pick a fight but are irritated about something different? Looking back, how many fights have you had over little things that do not really matter? What was the real problem? Did you ever discuss it or solve it?

To identify the problem, and to clarify the issues, you must first look to yourself. Why do you feel upset? Why do you feel threatened? How do you define this problem? *The solution begins with you.*

Our natural tendency is to justify our actions and blame our spouse. We ask ourselves, "Why does he act that way?" We then give ourselves answers based on our perceptions. Through mind-reading, reading the future, and often labeling our spouse in our mind with attributes like immature, neurotic, and so on, we are ready for the next fight. See how many dirty fighting techniques we have already used? We call this judging, and the Lord has been clear about judging: "Judge not that ye be not judged."

To clarify some of your own perceptions, stop now and ask yourself some different questions:

Why do you feel threatened by your mate's behavior?
Does it go against expectations you had about love and relationships?

Were these realistic expectations?

Where do they come from?

Are they related to your father or mother?

Do they really apply in this case?

Is your spouse really doing this to spite you?

Is there some other explanation?

Have you ever clarified this issue in the past?

For example, your credit card is almost full, money is tight, and your husband forgot to pay the monthly allotment on time. This means a surcharge and that you cannot use that card as planned. This is not the first time that he has been late paying the bills or irresponsible about money. You are furious. Your natural reaction is to start labeling him as irresponsible, or worse. This is a problem. Will yelling at him and calling him names change something? Is that how we are able to change others, through anger and criticism?

What can you do differently?

We must first clarify our own perceptions and expectations *before* we confront our spouse. Very often, we may find that the problem is with us, not our spouse. Are we using words like *should* to define our spouse's behavior? The word *should* is usually an indication that we are using convergent thinking. We are defining our companion's behavior by our standards that feel right. In this case, is it "bills *should* be paid on time," or "money *should* be spent wisely"? Another way to find out if we reacting to our own expectations is to examine our automatic thoughts. That is, what do we say to ourselves when we are angry? What is the belief or attitude that accompanies that thought? Does it begin with something similar to "If he really loved me, he wouldn't do that"? On the other hand, "If she cared, she wouldn't do that." Is the belief relevant to your situation? Are you saying, "If he really cared about our marriage, he would pay bills on time and not waste money"? Does your spouse see things from the same perspective? What are other explanations for the same behavior? Is your spouse's behavior caused by cultural differences? What was his or her upbringing? Did punctuality and money have the same importance as it did in your family? Is it due to gender? Did your family have money problems when you were young and you have a lot of insecurity about money? Have you communicated this to your mate? We have covered many of these issues in previous chapters. When we are sincere and honest with ourselves, we often resolve the conflict by changing our perceptions.

Your answers to some of the above questions might be, "Of course being responsible about money is important," and "Yes, he is irresponsible." Let us take it a step further, however. Why do you give him the responsibility of paying the bills? Is it because your father did it in your family and this is a "manly thing to do"? Are you comparing him to your father? Is this fair or right? Was your father this responsible at twenty-five, or did he learn over the years so that by the time you were a young woman and noticed these things, he had learned? Maybe the simplest solution is for you to pay the bills.

Seeing things from another perspective requires asking the right questions. Not everyone is equally competent at self-analysis, nor can everyone empathize and put themselves in their spouse's shoes with equal ease. Both these qualities can, however, improve with practice. When the Lord asks us to pray often and pray for all our necessities, praying to ask for His help in examining our own feelings and reactions seems most appropriate. Ask the Lord to better see the "beams" in your eyes so that you can grow and overcome some your mistaken and unrealistic perceptions.

A second step in self-analysis is examining needs and separating them from desires. Needs are things that are necessary for our emotional, physical, spiritual, or psychological development. Desires are things that we would like but with which we can do without. I may *need* to find a way to relax, but I *desire* a trip to Bermuda to achieve this. In a conflict, needs cannot be negotiated because we cannot thrive if they are not being met. Desires, however, can be compromised. The better we are able to separate our needs from our desires, the easier the next steps of the conflict resolution become. It is also useful to concentrate on what we think our spouse's needs and desires are too so that we can clarify these when we start the discussion. Questions like, "What would happen if I didn't have this, or do this?" or "How would I be damaged if I don't get what I am asking for?" can help clarify our desires and needs. Try picturing your life in the relationship over the next month or year if you do not obtain what you say you need. Have you clarified those needs to your spouse?

Often we look at our needs and not our companion's needs. Even more frequently, we do not examine the relationship's needs. What are our shared needs? How do you need each other in order for you and your relationship to be strengthened and improved? What do you need to do together to improve the relationship? How can you achieve that in this conflict situation? Too often, we solve conflict by satisfying the needs of one or the other spouse at the cost of harming or strangling the relationship. When we realize that we want to work together to achieve certain goals, then individual conflicts become less important than the overall relationship. This is true in business, in international politics, in the family with the children, and above all between soul mates. At this point, we also have shared power—the power of the couple to achieve their goals.

Once we have reflected on and clarified our own perceptions and expectations and we have meditated about our needs, our companion's needs, and our shared needs, then we can confront our spouse with the objective of finding a solution that will solve the problem and strengthen the couple. There are helpful rules of engagement that make the discussion less confrontational. These are factors like choosing the timing and location of the discussion. To begin a discussion in the middle of a football game that you know your husband wants to see, or after a long day for your wife, is not going to help. The real issue is that, if we want to find, in good faith, a solution to our mutual problem and not just show our spouse that we are right, we will do everything possible to render the atmosphere appropriate for both parties to have a discussion.

What is even more important is that we explain our position without putting our spouse on the defensive. Psychologists advise the use of "I" language, or better. "I feel" language. Rather than asking, "Why do *you*," or "When *you*," begin with "*I* feel." An argument that my wife and I had for years might demonstrate the difference. I have a deep booming voice, and when I get excited or angry, the tone of my voice increases. Whenever we had any type of discussion, the tone of my voice would increase without my realization, and my wife would begin to interrupt the conversation and say, "Lower your voice!" This would do nothing but irritate me more, and it was more likely that the tone of my voice would increase rather than decrease. After months or years of this, she would begin with, "Why do you always have to raise your voice?" or "Why are you always so angry?" Naturally, I would defend myself, or counterattack, and the discussion would go on. Finally, one day, whether by accident or on purpose, my wife explained that when I raise my voice, she always gets the feeling that I am angry with her and she becomes afraid. She went on to explain how this fear was probably caused by experiences she had in her family as a child. What could I say? Was there anything to defend—I was not under attack; she was just explaining the reason that she has the reaction she does. For the first time, I had some understanding of the problem, and we started actively searching for a solution. This is "I feel" language. I can only do this if I have done the work to first clarify my own perceptions.

Often conflict will resolve itself at this stage when each spouse explains their perceptions and intentions in a way that lets the other person understand their feelings. This is when misunderstandings are clarified, and often the first step is to bring to the surface past experiences that distort or cloud our vision. When there are still differences, it is necessary to pass on to the next phase of searching for a solution.

The best way to get a good idea is to get many ideas.[3]
—Linus Pauling, Noble Prize for chemistry

If our typical convergent thinking has led us into the conflict trying to decide who is right and who is wrong, then we need something else to solve the conflict. This is "divergent thinking" and is just the opposite. If convergent thinking leads us to narrow down the options until we come up with one solution, divergent thinking means opening up the options to many solutions, as seen below.

This is the creative approach to finding a solution that best resolves the problem for both spouses and fortifies the relationship because you work

Problem

Divergent thinking

Many solutions

together on the solution of the problem. There are several techniques that experts use in business or for team groups and that are equally appropriate in the relationship. The best known is brainstorming. There are three steps to brainstorming, but the first is the most important. This is moment of divergent thinking—coming up with as many solutions as possible without any logical or critical evaluation. There are two ways of doing this. In business when a creative solution is required, a group of people who are working on the problem get together around a table and just start throwing out ideas. They are encouraged to come up with the most wild and stupid idea they can think of, and no one is allowed to comment or criticize the ideas expressed. Often, the most absurd idea becomes the basis of the solution. The group nominates a secretary to write everything down.

The second step of critically evaluating the concepts occurs after the group expresses all the ideas. A couple or a family can follow this same approach. The advantage of this approach is that hearing other people's ideas can spark creative ideas and lead it in new directions. A disadvantage to this approach, however, is that when there are one or two dominate people in the group, often the whole group is influenced by their ideas, and the thinking goes off in just one or two directions. To avoid this, some groups use brain writing. In this case, each person in the group writes down one idea on a sheet of paper and then passes it to someone else who will add an idea sparked by the original idea. This then is exchanged with someone else, until everyone has added at least one idea on the sheet of everyone else in the group. This way hundreds of ideas can be generated. This can be adapted to the couple in two ways. Each can begin with a sheet of paper, write their ideas, and exchange the sheets back and forth, until they have exhausted their ideas. Better, each can write down on separate index cards as many ideas as they can. This way they each have several ideas to begin with and they can pass the cards back and forth adding ideas each time. Another solution may be to get help from family or friends to form a larger group.

We can use literally dozens of techniques to enhance creative thought. Most of them use either free association like brainstorming where we allow our thoughts to roam or force associations in which we take two unrelated concepts and try to find an analogy or connection. One example of this is *brutethink* that was explained in chapter five. Another is called the Circle of Opportunity. To use this you need a pair of dice. Follow these six steps:

1. State the problem or challenge you want to solve.
2. Draw a circle and number it like a clock from one to twelve.
3. Select the twelve most important aspects or attributes of the challenge, and write them next to each of the numbers in your circle.
4. Throw one die to find the first attribute to focus on.
5. Throw both dice to choose the second aspect.
6. Consider the attributes both separately and together. Free-associate each aspect and how to connect the two to find a solution to your problem. The free associations can lead you to any other concept or attribute that you can think of.
7. Search for a link between your associations and your challenge.[4]

The purpose of this or any other method is to help us use divergent thinking to solve our problem and overcome our frozen thinking patterns. Working together to create new approaches to solving problems can also provide the couple with shared power and the ability to work together to overcome obstacles.

The principle is that there are no pre-established right answers but only the best possible solution that allows the couple to fulfill each other's needs and their shared needs. Because we live in an age of constant change, each couple has to find their own answers to solve life's problems. The more creative we can learn to be, the better we can become in overcoming life's challenges.

The Lord has not left us alone in this process. The difference between this church and all others is that we believe in personal revelation. We believe that when we are searching for the right solution in harmony with the Spirit, we have a right to the help of the Lord. The Lord can help us in each stage of conflict resolution. We can call upon Him in prayer to help find the best solution for our marriage. Too often we tend to pray to the Lord for help, and forget how revelation works. We have to do all the work to find what we believe is the best solution, and then He will confirm it in our hearts and minds (see D&C 9).

Remember that in our garden it is the contrast between the plants that renders both more beautiful. It is not by changing the other, attacking it, or pulling it up by the roots that we solve something. We each have to find the room for our own growth for our roots to grow in respect with our spouse's. We both need sunshine, water, and nutrients, and we should work together to obtain our needs so that both plants can grow and blossom.

NOTES

1. Phillip C. McGraw, PhD, *Life Strategies, Doing What Works, Doing What Matters* (New York: Hyperion, 1999).
2. Peter H. Neidig, *Family Advocacy Domestic Violence Prevention Program Volume II* (Beaufort, SC: Behavioral Science Associates, 1998).
3. Roger von Oech, *A Whack on the Side of the Head* (Stamford, Connecticut: US Games System, Inc., 1990), 28.
4. Michael Michalko, *Thinkertoys* (Berkeley, California: Ten Speed Press, 1991), 181.

Rule 8

KINDLE THE FLAME

For this cause shall a man leave father and mother, and shall cleave to his wife: and they twain shall be one flesh? Wherefore they are no more twain, but one flesh. What therefore God had joined together, let not man put asunder.

—Matthew 19:5–6

There is probably no topic that is discussed more in our society than sex. We are all experts, and yet the majority of couples rate their sex life as so-so. It is one of the major disappointments of a relationship, and extramarital affairs are still one of the major causes of divorce. Why?

How is it possible that even though we are bombarded with sexual messages, many still find sex boring? Is sexual routine and boredom a necessary part of marriage? What can we do to keep our romantic love alive? How can we keep the spark alive?

The first message is that sex is not love and love is not sex. A relationship built exclusively on good sex is eventually doomed unless a deeper rapport somehow develops. We previously mentioned that teenagers marry because of passionate love and infatuation. Within two years, as the passion and reality sets in, they often divorce. They did not fall in love with each other but rather with the idea of love and the fantasy they created. The passion was inflamed by lust and devoured in sex, but nothing real and lasting was created from these flames. These are bedmates, not soul mates!

On the other hand, to have a spiritual and intellectual bond and nothing more is more enduring but unfulfilling. Making love is and should be the nonverbal, physical expression of the love and affection we have for each other. It is a physical bonding that expresses the deep inner feelings of cherishing, love, and passion. It renders real and concrete the spiritual and emotional bonding that we have created, and it goes far beyond just sex! It must permeate our lives and our relationship. It is a constant search for new ways to give pleasure to our spouse, to know him or her intimately in a way that no one else imagines. It is giving ourselves up to our spouse because we trust him or her fully. It is love.

Our church leaders have been clear that sex is not just for procreation but that it is a deep expression of love between husband and wife that brings them closer both emotionally and physically. President Kimball said:

> *In the context of lawful marriage, the intimacy of sexual relations is right and divinely approved. There is nothing unholy or degrading about sexuality in itself, for by that means men and women join in a process of creation and in an expression of love.[1]*

> *Marriage is not just for sexual activity, of course, but this union provides a profound way for each spouse to express love and commitment. Sexual intercourse was designed by Deity to be a physical, emotional, and spiritual union that fulfills our deepest desires for intimacy within the context of marriage. Just as a good marriage increases sexual libido, so also do satisfactory sexual relations confer soul-strengthening emotions on both spouses.[2]*

> —Douglas E. Brinley

> *Sex is for procreation and expression of love. It is the destiny of men and women to join together to make eternal family units. In the context of lawful marriage, the intimacy of sexual relations is right and divinely approved.[3]*

> —Spencer W. Kimball, *Teachings*, 311

And again:

> *Husband and wife . . . are authorized, in fact they are commanded, to have proper sex, when they are married for time and eternity.[4]*

> —Kimball, *Teachings*, 312

Sexual relations can be the barometer of a relationship. If our sex life is boring and routine, it is likely that everything else in our relationship is boring and routine too. If our spouse is selfish during sex, he or she probably is the same way in most other relationship issues. The wife who is always frustrated and cannot express her sexual desires probably cannot communicate other needs that she has. The couple that cannot compromise and agree on household chores may have difficulty finding harmony and unity in sex. Our sexual life is not divorced from who we are and the relationship we have created; it is the physical expression of that same relationship.

In the same way, what happens in our sexual relations affects all other aspects of our relationship. Sexual dysfunctions like vaginismus, inhibited desire, premature ejaculation, or erectile dysfunction—whether originating from physical or psychological causes—generate tension and misunderstandings that can poison trust and cause frustrations. Inadequate or negative sexual education, misunderstanding of gender differences in sexual response, and poor communication can make the most loving relationship frustrating and unsatisfying. Just like any aspect of our relationship, good lovemaking requires effort, knowledge, and creativity.

What can be done to keep lovemaking interesting? How can we find new ways to demonstrate the physical and sexual bond that expresses love for our spouse? We need to address three aspects: understanding the sexual differences between male and females, communicating needs, and learning the art of love.

THE MICROWAVE AND THE WOOD OVEN

Take a minute and think about your sexual relationship with your spouse. On a scale from 0 to 10, where is your relationship?

0	1	2	3	4	5	6	7	8	9	1	0
None		*Poor Relationship*				*Sometimes Satisfying*				*Fantastic*	

What are some of the problems you perceive? How do you think your relationship could improve?

Now read the following section to understand the gender differences, and try to see how much of the problem is caused by physiological differences between you and your mate.

There are few areas where the differences between men and women are so misunderstood as in the sexual realm. If we divide the human sexual response into the three phases—desire, excitement, and orgasm—we find that there are major gender differences in all three. As we stated in the previous chapter, all these differences are generalizations and may not apply to everyone, but they are usually true.

DESIRE STAGE

The desire stage of the human sexual response is the most complex because it is controlled by our higher brain and includes all of our attitudes, beliefs, and experiences. Hormones and other physiological reactions also influence desire. In animals, hormones play a major role, and sex is mostly instinctual, intended for procreation. Humans are more evolved, but we cannot ignore the role of hormones in the desire stage. Sexual desire in the brain is produced by androgens (male sexual hormones) that are present in both men and women and is somewhat inhibited by estrogen (the female hormone). In men, testosterone is present in high quantities, and the body works to keep it at a stable rate. There is far less testosterone in women, and the output is not as stable. There is more estrogen. It is not the amount of the hormone flowing through the body that creates the difference in desire between men and women because the female's brain is far more sensitive to the testosterone that is present. Rather, it is the fluctuation of the hormone in the woman that creates many differences.

Sex allows a man to feel his needs for love, while receiving love helps a woman to feel her hunger for sex.[5]

—John Gray, *Mars and Venus in the Bedroom*

In men, whether they are tired, stressed, angry, or hungry, there is little variation in the testosterone in their bloodstream, at least in the short term. Therefore, their desire does not decrease. This is why a man, even if he is tired at the end of the day, can still desire sex. Or, if he just fought with his wife and is angry, he may still have the desire. In addition, men accumulate sperm and seminal fluid, and as the amount increases, it triggers the brain and increases sexual desire so that there can be release.

Small changes in the hormone level in women, instead, can make a large difference in the brain's stimulation of sexual desire. Thus, when a woman is tired, stressed, or angry, there is a drop in the hormonal level, and her desire diminishes drastically. Since the androgens and estrogen in her blood also vary with her menstrual period, there are times when she has little desire, usually at the beginning of her period. Desire will increase dramatically during the middle of her menstrual cycle when she is most fertile and then diminish again.

External factors also influence the brain hormones. Studies have found, for example, that men isolated in military or scientific sites in the Arctic or in Alaska who have no possibility of sexual expression have a dramatic drop in their level of testosterone. Therefore, when there are no sexual stimuli, the body compensates and lowers the amount of hormones and consequently the level of desire. It then increases dramatically a few days before the men go on leave. In a relationship, when there is little sexual expression, desire will also drop. The less sex that is possible, the less hormonal desire is present. Just the opposite is also true, and the more sex the couple engages in, the more they will desire sex. In couples that suffer from inhibited desire, one of the best remedies is to increase the sexual expression.

Finally, hormonal levels vary with age. In men, testosterone levels are highest at ages eighteen to twenty and gradually diminishes over the years with significant drops in their thirties and again in their fifties. In women, estrogen levels that inhibit desire decreases with significant drops in their thirties. Androgen production increases after thirty. Most women enjoy sex and desire it more in their late thirties and forties than earlier. As a result of this, we find that the greatest difference in desire is early in life when men in their teens or twenties are at their highest level and women are at their lowest. As time passes, there is convergence of desire, and finally there is often an inversion in which men in their forties and fifties are concerned with other issues, and their wives complain that their husbands are "dead batteries."

These hormonal aspects are compounded by other factors. Men are turned on by visual stimuli and fantasy. Women are turned on by tactile stimulus and fantasy. In general, many women do not understand how powerful visual stimulus can be for men, and most men do not understand the woman's need for touch. This need transcends sex. A woman needs to be touched, caressed, hugged, and held every day—several times a day. Touch for the woman is love made manifest. Many women engage in sex just for the physical closeness it generates, not for sexual release. Unfortunately, most men do not understand this, and being left-hemisphere-oriented, they go right for the objective—orgasm.

The fantasies of men and women are different. We can see it in literature and entertainment. Men and women have very different tastes to the point that many women do not enjoy men's books or movies and vice versa. Most men prefer reading adventure novels or seeing action films. These are graphic and fast moving. The typical plot is the man saving the world in some way and being a hero who women cannot resist. Beginning with James Bond and continuing to the present, the fantasy is that the man is irresistible and the woman cannot stay away from him. They all desire him and want to have sex with him.

The best-selling type of novel is the romance novel, read exclusively by women. I have never met a man who managed to read one. I have tried several times to read a Danielle Steele novel out of curiosity but have never made it to the end. It is boring! There is no action, and it does not appeal to the male fantasy. The female fantasy is about attraction and commitment. It is the dark, handsome stranger who cannot resist the woman and sweeps her off her feet. It is about all the attention and affection he gives her. She changes him, he ends his wanderings, and he can now see no one but her. Of course, in the end, she discovers that he is rich and powerful.

These fantasies describe the difference in the basic needs of men and women. We both need love but express it differently. Men need to feel needed. A man needs to feel that he is a hero for his wife. He is there to protect her and solve her problems. He needs to feel that he is competent and know that his wife respects this competency. He needs to be sexually validated. Sex, for the male, is part of his identity and self-esteem. When his wife rejects him sexually, he feels rejected as a male. The female, instead, needs to feel that her husband desires her and perceives that she is unique. She needs to know that, because she is special, he will commit to her and long to be with her. She changes the beast into a caring person who can be strong in the world but tender with her.

Another difference is that men desire sex for release and relaxation, whereas women need to be able to relax to enjoy sex. Men become more intimate after sex when they can relax, while women need to relax to feel pleasure. This often places men and women at cross-purposes. She wants to finish cleaning the kitchen and get the housework done so she can relax and enjoy the companionship of sex. He wants to have sex now so he can discharge the tensions of the day and relax.

It is not just at the physical level that differences exist but in relationships and past experience too. Remember that it is the higher brain that controls desire. Even if the hormonal level is low but I feel particularly close to my mate, my brain still triggers desire. Inversely, the hormonal level may be very high, but if I am angry with my spouse or worried about the children, there is no desire. Here too there are major differences between the sexes. Men tend to perceive sex as a physical release and source of pleasure divorced from the relationship. Women are predisposed to experience emotions and seek out relationships, and this becomes the important part of sexual expression. Women can experience sex as just a temporary physical pleasure, but usually they closely link the quality of the sexual experience to the quality of the relationship. When they feel neglected, unappreciated, or used in the relationship, there is little desire to manifest their love through sex.

Past experiences also influence desire, and again, it is more likely that a woman has had more negative experiences than a man. The three most important influences are sex education, first sexual experiences, and childhood sexual abuse or rape. Many girls, even today, arrive at their first menses without knowing what is happening to them. It is frightening. In our society, we perceive menstruation as something negative—the curse. As a result, female sexuality begins with a negative attitude. The sexual education of many girls is "don't do it!" Sex is describe as something dirty or frightening or both. The woman has to worry about pregnancy. She is at much higher risk for STDs, and the consequences of sex are more severe. In general, sex, for women, is strongly linked to worries and anxieties. Women are aware that recreational sex always has the potential for procreation. Early sexual experiences of most girls are often tainted with anxieties and are extremely disappointing. In one study, only 8 percent of women interviewed experienced an orgasm in their first sexual encounter whether before or after marriage. The most common reaction that they reported was, "Is this it? Is this all there is to sex?" This then is mixed with feelings of guilt and worries about pregnancy. Often sexual education for the woman describes sex as just a duty. Can duty ever be pleasure? Thus, for most girls, they have an education and early experiences that link sexual experience with guilt, anxiety, and disappointment.

As a result, obeying the law of chastity protects a young woman from many of the negative aspects of early sexual experiences. Just the same, many young women continue to receive a sexual education based on fear, guilt, and anxiety rather than on knowledge and choices.

How different this is for men. They receive little sexual education in the home, and the attitude of society and their peers is, "Go for it!" Most boys, after their first sexual experience, describe it with words like *fantastic, great,* or *unbelievable.* It is often linked to emotions of power, elation, and joy. They have scored; they have proven themselves a man; they have conquered. Our young men need a sexual education based on self-restraint and respect for women.

Community surveys in the United States have found that about one in three women were sexually abused as children. Many women report that they were subject to date rape or attempted rape by their boyfriends. Over half of all women in the United States have either been abused or raped, or experienced an attempted rape. How traumatic this is for the woman depends much on many factors such as who did it, how often it occurred, how old she was, and her sense of being responsible. Overall, however, it means that for many women, maybe even a majority, sex is not linked to pleasure at all. It is associated with bad memories of abuse and male dominance, negative emotions of fear, anxiety, or depression, and is aggravated by any problem in the relationship.

Sexual abuse of males also exists and can be equally traumatic, but it just does not happen as often. Surveys indicate that about 14 percent of males have experienced some form of sexual abuse as children. The most common long-term effect of sexual abuse in both sexes is inhibited sexual desire. Victims have a hard time establishing trust and intimacy, and sexual contact often brings back memories of the abuse.

The most common cause of inhibited sexual desire is depression, and often depression is a result of earlier abuse. It is not by chance that far more women suffer from chronic depression than do men. As the number of depressed people increases, the more sexual problems there will be in relationships. Unfortunately, many common anti-depressants such as Prozac further decrease sexual desire in many cases. Certainly, inhibited sexual desire is the most common sexual dysfunction and the most complex to treat, but it is not the only difference between men and women.

EXCITEMENT STAGE

Even if the differences of the excitement stage are fewer and less complicated than that for desire, they explain some of the major misunderstandings between men and women. In both men and women, vasocongestion and myotonia cause sexual arousal and excitement. Myotonia is an increase of muscle tension throughout the body that will escalate until orgasm explosively releases it. Vasocongestion means that once we receive a sexual stimulus, blood rushes to the genital area. In men, this is most evident as blood floods the spongy tissue of the penis and causes erection. It is the hydraulic pressure of the increased blood flow that causes erection. In women, the same thing happens. The inner and outer lips of the vagina and the clitoris are also made of spongy tissue, which engorge and harden in the same way. The inner lips of the vagina will double or even triple in size. The only difference is that it is less visible. As the tissues engorge, they become more sensitive, and pleasure increases. Thus, the physiological process is the same for men and women. The difference is how long this stage lasts.

In healthy young men, it only takes seconds for erection to occur when they perceive a visual stimulus and their fantasy is triggered. When erection takes place, it only takes a few minutes of stimulation before men are ready for orgasm. This depends to some extent on age and health and will increase as men age and their circulatory system is less efficient. But even so, it rarely takes more than ten minutes. For a man, the time of the initial stimulus to when he is ready for orgasm may take anywhere from seconds to a few minutes. He may begin by massaging his wife's back, with no other idea in mind. But as soon as she gives some signal that she is receptive, he is almost instantly excited and stimulated. The man is a microwave oven! It takes but a few minutes to cook him from the inside out.

In Italy, a wood oven is used to make a good pizza. The wood oven provides a uniform heat and flavors the crust in a unique way. The oven has to be stoked and fired at least an hour before cooking to allow the wood to create the coals perfect for cooking. Just as the male is a microwave, the woman is a wood oven. She has to be slowly sparked and allowed to burn until her coals are ready to cook. Then she is ready to add her special flavor to the meal.

Few men realize how different women are. The woman excites more gradually. She is ready to burn only if she can relax, has liberated herself from other worries, and can focus on enjoying the pleasure of the sexual stimulation and companionship. She can begin excitement immediately just as the man does, but she needs tactile stimulation for much longer before she is ready for orgasm. In a woman, this period can last from a few minutes to an hour, with the average being between twenty and thirty minutes. Very often for the couple, this means the man is stimulated, has an erection, and ejaculates before she is even warm. It's no wonder that women complain that sex is too brief and there is no foreplay. Men do not need foreplay, and many do not realize that the woman does. The man who was in the kitchen massaging his wife's shoulders and feels her respond becomes instantly excited and wants sex right now—in the kitchen. In his mind, the kids are in front of the TV and sex is only a three-minute affair!

ORGASM STAGE

There are few differences between men and women during the orgasm stage, which is the physiological release of muscle tension accumulated during the excitement stage and consists of a series of contractions of the muscles in the genital area. It is usually accompanied by pleasure, release, and satisfaction. In the male, it is accompanied by ejaculation of the sperm and seminal fluid. The major difference is that the male needs time after ejaculation, called the refractory period, before he can experience orgasm and ejaculation again. This may vary from a few minutes to several hours depending on age, health, and the number of recent ejaculations. The woman instead needs no refractory period and may have another orgasm immediately. She may even have multiple orgasms.

These physiological differences inherently lead to misunderstandings in sexual expression between men and women. Typically, men do not understand the woman's need to relax to enjoy sex. For her this means not having to worry about the kitchen being a mess, the children interrupting, or the telephone ringing. She knows that she needs time to become excited; therefore, she will tend to desire sex when she knows the children are away or that she will be caught up with her work. Men also do not understand why, if she enjoys sex, she is reluctant to have it all the time. They do not understand that even in the best of circumstances, for her sexual intercourse is not just pleasure but is a responsibility. Did I take the pill? Will the condom slip off? When will I have my next period? Since men tend to separate the relationship from sex, they scarcely comprehend how closely intertwined these are for their wife. Even though a woman can desire sexual gratification and physical pleasure, she usually associates sexual expression with physical harmony in a relationship. If she does not feel in tune with her husband or if she feels neglected or unappreciated, there is little desire for sex.

President Hugh B. Brown said:

> Many marriages have been wrecked in the dangerous rocks of ignorant and debased sex behavior, both before and after marriage. Gross ignorance on the part of newlyweds on the subject of the proper place and functioning of sex results in much unhappiness and many broken homes. Thousands of young people come to the marriage altar almost illiterate insofar as this basic and fundamental function is concerned. . . . Some sound instruction in this area will help a man to realize the numberless, delicate differentiations and modifications in the life and reactions of the normal woman.[6]

This means that you men must learn that sex does not begin in the bedroom. Sex is an all-day affair. If you want to enjoy good sex with your wife, make sure that it is lovemaking. Make it an expression of love, and make sure that you have expressed love throughout the day and through the weeks in many other ways. Then, realizing that your wife needs to have things in order to be able to relax and enjoy sex, do the dishes and clean up, and put the children to bed. Do not do chores only on the nights that you want sex, or she will feel manipulated and will be turned off. However, the more you ease her load and show appreciation for her, the more she is receptive. Women's fantasies are about romance, not sex. You have to satisfy that need for romance for her to open to you sexually. Learn from her what pleases her physically. Remember her need to be touched and cuddled; do not make all physical contact sexual. Learn to control yourself to satisfy your mate. When was the last time that you found a babysitter for the kids and planned a romantic evening? When was the last time you took a trip together or did something special for her? Start today.

You women need to understand men's need for sexual validation. For a man, an intrinsic part of his male image is to be sexually attractive. Constant rejection or avoidance of intercourse diminishes his self-esteem and creates frustration. Remember also that a man wants to feel competent and needed, so teach him gently to be a good lover. Faking an orgasm or not correcting his clumsy stroking will deprive both of you of the emotional bonding of making love. Women need to know that just as they need time to relax and to enjoy sex, this is the exact opposite of what is natural for the male. For men, scheduled sex is better than nothing, but the epitome of pleasure is spontaneous sex. One of the major complaints that men have is that they always have to take the initiative, so they are always at risk for rejection. At the same time, one of the major fantasies of men is to be seduced. They want their wife to show interest, take the initiative, and seduce them.

It is evident that men and women are different, but just as was discussed earlier, differences can be either an advantage or a handicap depending on how we use them.

We must understand the differences, and we need to use them to grow. As men learn to open up and communicate their feelings, they learn to deepen their relationship and be more alive and aware of their own emotions and those of others. As they learn to control their sexual response, they prolong not only their spouse's pleasure but also their own. Men learn that sex is also lovemaking and can be a profound experience. As women overcome their anxieties and the idea that sex is a duty, they can experience the physical pleasure of sex. They can appreciate and enjoy the variety and spontaneity that men introduce. Both can grow and learn by understanding and drawing on the strengths of the other. To understand each other's differences, the first step is to communicate their needs.

COMMUNICATE NEEDS

Few of us had good sex education. Few of us had open discussions with our parents or peers about our sexual feelings, fears, or emotions. When we talked about sex with our friends, it was often to brag or belittle, but rarely was it an open, sincere conversation about our feelings. As a result, many couples have great difficulty opening up about their sexual desires and expectations. It is a modern paradox that the subject that is most talked about, displayed, and bandied about in public still remains taboo in private between many couples. Few of the couples I've seen in therapy have talked openly about their sexual fantasies or desires. There is no better time than today to begin. Try completing the following scheme, and give one to your spouse to complete.

My Romantic Evening

My romantic evening would begin at _____ o'clock, and I would like my husband to . . . _____

_____

_____

_____

_____

_____

_____

_____

_____

My Romantic Evening

My romantic evening would begin at _____ o'clock, and I would like my wife to . . . _____

_____

_____

_____

_____

_____

_____

_____

_____

The only rule to this exercise is to be as honest and creative as possible. Once you and your spouse have written out your ideal romantic evening, decide who will begin. Roll dice or flip a coin. The purpose of the exercise is to learn what pleases your spouse and to *begin* the process of providing pleasure. If your spouse isn't perfect in satisfying your fantasy the first or second time, maybe you need to be clearer. The beauty of this exercise is that you can and should repeat it regularly. Each time you can become more daring, and each time your spouse can become more creative in pleasing you.

You cannot just wish for romance; you must communicate your needs. One of the biggest myths that Hollywood has given women is, "If he really loved me, he would automatically understand my needs and satisfy them." It should be clear that we are all so unique that no one can fully know the needs or desires of the other person. Men and women are so different that most men don't have a clue about the desires of their wives, no matter how much they love them.

If you are honest with yourself, you must admit that your desires and even your needs fluctuate according to your mood, stress, or activity level. The proof of love is not that your husband can read your mind but that once you have clearly expressed a desire, he is willing to try to please you to the best of his abilities. Men and women often work on the false premise that "What I need is what you need, and what I desire is what you should desire." Therefore, men and women feel no need to communicate their needs because they think that their spouses are feeling or *should* be feeling the same way.

Finally, we do not express sexual needs and desires because it was taboo in our families growing up, and it often remains taboo in our minds. Many women feel that if they openly express desire for more sex, or sex that is more creative, their husbands will judge them somehow perverted, when most men would like nothing better. The social stigma of the loose woman who is oversexed still conditions our intimate relationships. Therefore, it is necessary to express what we want in a nonthreatening way.

Try this next exercise. Once again, you fill out one list, and let your spouse fill out another.

MY SEXUAL DESIRES

Romance   *Sex*

Five things I would like us to do together more often:
1.

2.

3.

4.

5.

Five things I think you would like me to do more often:
1.

2.

3.

4.

5.

Five things I would like you to do more often:
1.

2.

3.

4.

5.

Romance   *Sex*

Five things I would like us to do together more often:
1.

2.

3.

4.

5.

Five things I think you would like me to do more often:
1.

2.

3.

4.

5.

Five things I would like you to do more often
1.

2.

3.

4.

5.

Now compare your lists. Talk about what you wrote and explain what you would like. Listen to what your spouse would like. Experiment. You can and should repeat this exercise too so that each time you can find new ideas or techniques with which you would like to experiment. Making your sexual expression more creative and pleasurable requires that you learn more about it.

THE ART OF LOVE

Too often, the couple, when they first meet and fall in love, is full of passion. They enjoy sex and are creative. Then slowly, other aspects of reality intrude. Work and tending the children consume their energy and time, and sexual intercourse becomes something hurried or occasional to keep *him* satisfied. The couple finds one or two positions that are comfortable and starts settling into a routine that soon becomes boring. Several studies find that within three to five years of marriage, the average couple goes from having sexual intercourse twelve to fifteen times per month to about four to six times per month. The numbers may not be very accurate since every couple is different and most people lie on surveys, but the downward trend is mostly true. One should note that as the frequency of sexual intercourse declines, so too does the general satisfaction of the couple with their relationship. Sex is not just a physical release; it is an important expression of love. When we do not make time to reinforce our love physically or we do not make the effort to do it in a way that is pleasing and satisfying to our spouse, then the relationship suffers.

The man who uses his hands is a laborer
The man who uses his hands and his head is a craftsman
The man who uses his hands, head, and heart is an artist.[7]

—Anonymous

Good sexual expression is an art. It requires that we learn the techniques that provide pleasure for our spouses and that we give with our hearts. It also means being open and appreciative to receive from our spouse and to participate physically and emotionally in this act of mutual pleasure and confirmation.

All artists must master the elements of their medium of expression. The photographer must learn all the functions of the camera. He must learn how the image in the camera is different from the image of his eye. He must learn about filters and lighting and how to develop the film, use contrast, and experiment with different films and paper. The novelist must learn the medium of language, the rhythm and flow of words, the syntax and pragmatics of expression. The painter will work with all different mediums from watercolors to oil to charcoal and pencil drawing. He will draw human figures, animals, still life pictures, and landscapes for years before concentrating on his own style. Once the artist has thoroughly absorbed the medium of expression and then the creative vision, the innovative techniques and the unique perception of the world can emerge. Now the artist can transmit to others his true passion. Is sex any different?

If I have great passion but do not learn to express that in a way that gives joy to my spouse, I have labored at love, but there was no art. We must first learn the physical, psychological, and emotional needs of our spouse, and we must learn the physiology and anatomy of sexual expression.

Remember also that sex is not just sex but lovemaking. There are craftsmen who know the techniques and apply them well but without heart. The best lovemaking is always between two committed spouses who love and respect each other, know each other's physical and emotional needs, and have learned to give pleasure in unique ways to that person. Lovemaking should get better as the relationship grows and deepens. The best lovemaking should be between soul mates!

Read marriage and sex manuals together. Discuss what you prefer or what you disagree with. On the other hand, read the manuals separately and surprise your beloved with something new. Surprise is the antithesis of boredom. Keep your spouse guessing what is going to happen next time. There are numerous articles in every major woman's magazine about sexual expression. Read them together and experiment. Remember, however, that the greatest expert on what gives pleasure to your spouse is your spouse. Respect his or her choices. Discover his or her pleasure points.

Because men and women are so different in their physical and emotional reactions, it is necessary to learn their language of lovemaking. Have you ever noticed when traveling to foreign countries that if you ask a question in English, the natives may answer in their own language? They will speak slowly or loudly as though talking to a child or a dunce. But it makes no difference. If you do not know the language, you cannot understand or make yourself understood. Is it any different for lovemaking? If you cannot express your love in your spouse's language, your intention may be good, but your spouse has not received the message. If you cannot express your physical love in a way that is pleasing and exciting for your spouse, has he or she received the message? Or have you communicated only your selfish needs?

Just as reason is linked with emotion and to divide one from the other is to lose a portion of the whole, so is our spirit linked to our physical body. We cannot and should not nourish one and forget the other or we remain spiritually or physically handicapped. To nourish our spiritual union and ignore the physical and emotional is to deny that the spirit and body are united into an eternal soul. It is through the physical love we express to our wife or husband that we can feel at one with them and unite physically and spiritually.

In our garden we are uplifted through all of our senses. The visual beauty of the flowers and shrubs, the contrast of the colors, the fragrance of the flowers in bloom, the rustling of the wind through the leaves of the trees, and the texture of the moist soil engulf us. All these sensations heighten our appreciation of the beauty of the garden and lift our spirits to be grateful to the Lord for the beauty of nature. So too by sharing physical pleasure with our mate, by providing a release and joy, and by giving to each physically, we enhance the spiritual union that binds us.

> *I belong to my lover, and his desire is for me. Come my lover, let us go to the countryside, let us spend the nights in the villages. Let us go early to the vineyards to see if the vines have budded, if their blossoms have opened and if the pomegranates are in bloom—there I will give you my love.*
>
> —See The Song of Solomon 7:10–12

NOTES
1. Spencer W. Kimball, *The Teachings of Spencer W. Kimball*, Edward L. Kimball, ed. (Salt Lake City: Bookcraft, 1982), 311.
2. Douglas E. Brinley, *Marital Intimacy: A Sacred Key to a Successful Marriage.* Found in Daniel K . Judd, ed., *Living a Covenant Marriage: Practical Advice From 13 Individuals Who've Walked in Your Shoes.* Cited from LDS Library 2006, LDS Media Deseret Book.
3. Kimball, ibid., 311.
4. Ibid, 312.
5. John Gray, PhD, *Mars and Venus in the Bedroom* (New York: HaperCollins Publishers, 1995), 2.
6. Hugh B. Brown, *You and Your Marriage* (Salt Lake City: Bookcraft, 1960), 73–74.
7. W. Masters, V. Johnson, and R. Kolodny, *Human Sexuality* (Boston: Little, Brown & Co., 1985).

Rule 9

Nurture the Spirit

Whatever principle of intelligence we attain unto in this life, it will rise with us in the resurrection. And if a person gains more knowledge and intelligence in this life through his diligence and obedience than another, he will have so much the advantage in the world to come.
—Doctrine and Covenants 130:18–19

The meaning of earthly existence is not, as we have grown used to thinking, in prosperity, but in the development of the soul.[1]
—Alexander Solzhenitsyn

A relationship cannot grow unless each person in the relationship matures and develops. This means that, as we emotionally bond and dedicate ourselves to one another, there must also be space for individuality and time for our own development. The sign of a healthy relationship is that both members of the couple are evolving. This means that there has to be time and space for each of us to nurture our souls. There is a time to share activities as a couple, but there must be space to follow our individual goals. We and only we are responsible for our growth. If the forsythia grows and the Japanese peach blossom does not, soon the forsythia will overwhelm and hide the Japanese peach blossom. They are no longer in symbiosis adding to the other, but rather, one now shuts out the light and absorbs all the nourishment. Each plant may have different timing in its growth, but it has to be a reciprocal process.

As soul mates, we need to grow and to expand our conscious awareness of ourselves, the world around us, and of each other. As we deepen our understanding and increase our abilities, we can share at a more profound level with our soul mate. Not only that, but as we realize the importance of this process, we will delight in the progress and development of our beloved as she or he expands and grows. We must actively encourage and sustain the growth of our spouse because we know that we too will benefit. This is quite different from criticizing and telling them what to do. Too often, the forsythia would like the Japanese peach blossom to be just like him with the same yellow flowers, or the Japanese tree blossom wants the forsythia to produce the same fruit. Each plant and each person must expand and progress according to their own rhythm and their inner needs and potential. We cannot grow for them, and we cannot force them to grow. The more we try, the less they develop. Criticism is the acid that burns and destroys development; instead, encouragement and trust are the nutrients of growth. Each person must find their own path, and each person must strive to overcome and fulfill their destiny. But it is the spouse who loves us and believes in us that will nourish and sustain our growth.

To grow is defined in the dictionary as "to spring up and come to maturity; to be able to grow: thrive, to unite by . . . growth, . . . to increase, expand, and become."[2] An acorn planted in fertile ground that receives sunshine and water will grow to become a mighty oak tree. It has matured, thrived, expanded, and become what it was destined to be. It has reached its full potential. So the walnut becomes a walnut tree that spreads its branches, provides shade, and produces more nuts, and the tomato seed thrives and becomes a healthy tomato plant. Each plant, given the proper circumstance will grow, mature, and become what nature intended for it. So too we find in the animal kingdom.

Who are we? What does it mean to be mature? What do we expand to, and whom do we become? How do we grow? How do we reach our full potential?

You have already answered many of these questions when you wrote your goals for this life. Go back and consider what you wrote. It is legitimate that some goals we have for ourselves and for our relationships are concerned with this temporal and material sphere of life. Living in a nice home and having economic security may provide us the base to better achieve our potential, but they are not the ultimate goal. Rising in our career and advancing to higher positions may give us needed recognition and prestige, but even these are not the ultimate goal. We are human *beings*, not human *possessors* or human *doers*. Unfortunately, modern society judges people by what they own, by their bank account, or at least by the appearance of what they own. Are we happy? No, we are the country, with Japan, with the highest stress levels resulting in physical and mental health problems. Clinical depression has tripled in the last twenty years. External rewards, society's judgment, accolades from the public, keeping up with the Joneses, or acquiring money will never be truly satisfying. Finding joy from worldly sources means putting the evaluation of who you are and what you are worth into someone else's hands, and therefore you are dependent on them for your feelings of self-worth.

This concept is extremely important because it calls for a shift in our priorities. It is not what we achieve as far as position, recognition, or salary that has the most importance but how that job allows us to learn, to grow, and to enhance our abilities. The woman who stays home with the children and feels frustrated because she is not *achieving* anything and is falling behind in her career goals is instead passing through one of life's greatest challenges—rearing children. In no other job do we learn so much about ourselves and are we so stimulated to grow as in our role as parents. We learn to put aside our desires and give selflessly to the development of another human being twenty-four hours a day for at least eighteen years! What better training for growth? If the mother who is overwhelmed by dirty diapers and screaming children can realize how this deepens her understanding of love and her capacity to give, she will be less frustrated. The man who avoids dealing with the children deprives himself of a necessary growing experience. The parents who are exhausted in the evening but still make the effort to help their children with homework, put up with their tantrums, and still remain civil have learned discipline and emotional control in the hardest school of life. We must be aware of those experiences that are building our strengths and increasing our spiritual insight to better appreciate them and to keep our priorities straight. To do this we must first reflect on what spiritual growth is and then see how we can best pursue it.

The most important principle to remember is we are human beings and children of God. It is fulfilling our potential as a person and as a future god or goddess. It is who we are and who we become that determines our growth. It is fulfilling our potential as a person. It means transforming and changing ourselves into better people. It means we must rise to a higher plane of awareness and understanding. It means struggling to overcome our weaknesses and defects. This is spiritual growth.

The question then is, who do you want to *be*, not what do you want to achieve. Achievement is good if it contributes to the progress and growth of yourself or others, but it is not the same thing as spiritual growth. Who do you want to become? What type of person do you want to be five years from now, ten years from now, or at the end of your life? How can you transform yourself and live and grow at a higher plane? What does it mean to grow spiritually? This is something that each person must answer for himself, but here are some considerations. The scriptures are full of the qualities of a man of God:

> Put on therefore, as the elect of God, holy and beloved, bowels of mercies, kindness, humbleness of mind, meekness, longsuffering; Forbearing one another, and forgiving one another, if any man have a quarrel against any: even as Christ forgave you, so also do ye. And above all these things put on charity, which is the bond of perfectness. (Colossians 3:12–14)

Or again, in the Beatitudes we can find indications of who we should be spiritually and develop those traits:

Blessed are the poor in spirit whom come to the Lord.
Blessed are the meek.
Blessed are they who hunger and thirst after righteousness.
Blessed are the merciful.
Blessed are the pure in heart.
Blessed are the peacekeepers. (See Matthew 5:3–10.)

Some members of the Church find it difficult to quantify these spiritual qualities in their lives. We display some of these qualities some of the time, but we do not know where we are on a scale from one to ten. The question also remains, if, for example, I am not very meek, how do I develop meekness? In this respect, taking some of the theories from psychology may help us since many reflect the teachings of the gospel.

Many psychologists have tried to define aspects of human growth, and we may gain insight by considering their ideas. Psychologists use terms like *self-actualization, development, maturity,* and *psychological well-being,* though not the term *spiritual growth.* But in many cases, they are describing the same process. Although there are many differences in the theories, psychologists focus on five basic factors necessary for this process of self-actualization. These are selflessness, awareness or insight, self-control, openness to change, and personal responsibility. A principle, true of many theories, is that we are born with little ability in most of these aspects, but as we grow and develop, we become more capable and mature in each area. Some people, however, do not mature properly and remain psychological infants in one or more of these areas.

CONCERN FOR OTHERS

The process of development implies a moving away from a concern for self toward growing degrees of interest and concern for others. Another way to see this is to understand that we are born completely selfish. Babies know and are concerned only with the satisfaction of their own needs. As these needs are properly satisfied, they learn to satisfy the needs of others, and so they grow from selfishness to selflessness, from concern only for themselves to concern for others. One measurement of this is a person's ability to empathize with the troubles and sorrows of those around him and to actively act to help them. In other words, we learn to care and to love ourselves and others. We first express this in our family of origin, and then we learn to love our mates and are able to create an intimate relationship. Then as children arrive, we learn to give selflessly and to satisfy their needs. Through our work and interests, we enlarge our circle of influence and can touch the lives of an increasing number of people so that in the end, we extend our concern toward society and all humanity and we can direct our creative efforts to better the world.

> When you commit to a spiritual spouseship with another human being . . . you begin to form and to live by the values, perceptions, and actions that reflect equality with your spouse and a commitment to his or to her spiritual development and your own. You begin to set aside the wants of your personality in order to accommodate the needs of your spouse's spiritual growth, and, in doing that, you grow yourself. That is how a spiritual partnership works.[3]

The more we overcome our selfish desires and open up to others, the more empathetic we become. Empathy is the ability to feel the pain and joy of other people and to participate in their emotional life. For couples, it means that instead of getting angry because our spouse hasn't done something we wanted, we can put our self in their shoes and "feel" how tired or overwhelmed they are. Instead of being judgmental and criticizing because no one has fulfilled our needs, we become more loving and caring as we empathize with the needs and concerns of our beloved. This process implies that all activities that allow us, or force us, to overcome our selfish desires and increase our concern for others are for our growth and our own good. The Lord said clearly: " Love thy neighbor as thyself."

Spencer Kimball, speaking to a couple, also stated:

> For your love to ripen so gloriously, there must be an increase in confidence and understanding, a frequent and sincere expression of appreciation of one another. There must be a forgetting of self and a constant concern for the other.[4]

Where are you on this scale? Where is your spouse?

CONCERN AND EMPATHY

Selfish		Some concern for others				Selfless and altruistic			Empathetic	
0	1	2	3	4	5	6	7	8	9	10

AWARENESS

We also grow in awareness. The baby is concerned only for his needs because he cannot perceive others as separate from himself. The six-year-old child will give his father a toy car for Father's Day, not because he is self-serving but because he does not have the awareness of his father's desires as being different from his own. As we grow, we become aware of others and their different perceptions and needs. Many psychologists believe that this is the most defining quality of human growth: awareness of self and others. As has been stated, "know thyself and to thine own self be true."[5] The first step in this process is to know yourself. The purpose of many types of psychotherapies is to increase insight and self-awareness so that a person can gain control of his life. Can we have spiritual growth without this same insight?

Freud and his school of psychoanalysis have long emphasized that many of our feelings, emotions, and motivations remain unconscious. Freudians stress that the purpose of life is to become aware of these unconscious aspects, often originating in childhood, to gain control over yourself. We are empowered by self-awareness. We obtain self-control through understanding. We learn to properly use our emotions only if we are aware of our feelings and what triggers them. This self-awareness then leads to greater understanding and tolerance of others. We are now living at a higher plane of consciousness and insight. Just as the bird that soars higher sees farther, or the higher we climb the mountain the more we see of the surrounding landscape, so as we gain awareness, we increase the range of our understanding. We see our purpose in life and the motivations of others more clearly. We progress. Think of the quality of a relationship between two people who are totally aware and honest about their own feelings, motivations, and actions. They become two people who have no hidden agendas, no ulterior motives, who can live in full awareness of themselves, their mate, and the world around them.

And ye shall know the truth, and the truth shall set you free.

—John 8:32

And truth is knowledge of things as they are, and as they were, and as they are to come.

—Doctrine and Covenants 93:24

Can we ever be free from the shackles of our past unless we become aware of who we are and who we have been?

As we increase our insight into our motivations and feelings, we become more aware of the world around us. We start living more in the present and are at one with the world. There is the "two-minute rule" that states that most people spend 58 minutes of every hour fixated in the past or worrying about the future but spend only two minutes consciously aware of the present. Most memories that we ruminate from the past are sad and lead to depression, and the concerns of the future produce anxiety. The fact is that neither the past nor the future are reality. They are figments of our mental processes. It is only in the present that we can have awareness, that we can experience the world around us, and that we can be in contact with nature and other people. As we develop, we must stop letting experiences or future concerns drive us and learn to live in the present.

The wealth of a soul is measured by how much it can feel, its poverty by how little.[6]

—William R. Alger

What is your level of self-awareness? Are you in full contact with your feelings? Are you living in the present? Do you feel the sun or breeze on your skin as you walk? Are you in contact with nature, in harmony with the universe?

EMOTIONAL AND SPIRITUAL AWARENESS

Emotionally numb			*Aware of feelings*		*Totally aware of feelings*			*In harmony with universe*		
0	1	2	3	4	5	6	7	8	9	10

SELF-CONTROL

Another aspect of progress is self-control and . A man who has achieved wealth and recognition but throws a temper tantrum is a man who has not reached a higher spiritual plane. A man who is an esteemed scholar and statesman but cannot resist the temptation to cheat on his wife is still mired in lower levels of accomplishment. He has not even risen above the satisfaction of his physical needs. The term *emotional intelligence* that is now popular is based on the idea of self-control. Daniel Goleman, in his book *Emotional Intelligence,* defines it this way:

> Abilities such as being able to motivate oneself and persist in the face of frustrations; to control impulse and delay gratification, to regulate one's mood and keep distress from swamping the ability to think; to empathize and to hope.[7]

What is most fascinating about all the studies of emotional intelligence is that it is the number one factor in the success of a person. It is not necessarily the person who did well at school or who has a high IQ who gains success but rather the person who has learned and who can work with other people.

Self-control is spirituality![8]

—David O. McKay

It is in part through increased awareness and insight that we gain self-control. The more I understand why I behave certain ways, the more I am able to take control and change. It is not just emotional control that is necessary but in all aspects of life. Control of my actions often begins with control of my thoughts. In computer language, there is the saying, "Garbage in—garbage out!" Centuries ago it was equally stated, "As a man thinks in his heart so is he." Taking control of our lives means managing time wisely and starting to do those things that we know we should but for which we "never find the time." We must start eliminating bad habits so that we can live to our full potential.

There is probably no one quality more important in a loving relationship than self-control. The mate who spews out hateful and hurtful words when he is angry or who cannot help herself from constantly criticizing and nagging is damaging a precious relationship. We cannot express true love when there is no self-control. There is no spiritual growth when we are unable to reign in our physical needs and desires.

Spirituality equals . Where are you in this aspect of growth? Where is your spouse?

SELF-CONTROL

No self-control				*Occasional self-control*				*Total self-control in all areas*		
0	1	2	3	4	5	6	7	8	9	10

PERSONAL RESPONSIBILITY

Carl Rogers, another prominent psychologist, defined seven stages of development that focus on three fundamental elements: awareness (that we have discussed), openness to change, and responsibility. In the initial stage, he explains there is an unwillingness to talk about oneself, and personal feelings are neither recognized nor owned. The person is incapable of forming intimate relationships and does not recognize any problems as originating from himself. We call this person a "blamer." The problem is always someone or something else external to the person who takes no responsibility and has no desire to change. This stage of total closure is pathological and we hope few experience it. As we pass through the various levels we open, we become more aware of our feelings and those of others. We do not stop blaming the world for our problems until we reach the seventh stage.

This final stage represents a person who has progressed to total awareness of his own personal feelings and experiences, someone who lives in the present and who is not driven by past experiences or conflicts. It describes an individual who has overcome his own personal fears and anxieties and is completely open to new experiences and emotions. Such a person willingly engages in relationships with others and is capable of empathetic understanding. Finally, at this stage, the person is empowered and accepts responsibility for his actions and seeks to change his habits and behaviors to better himself and better his relationships. He perceives how he contributes to problems and seeks solutions within himself. Therefore, because of his awareness, he must also accept responsibility.

We are responsible for our behaviors, our thoughts, our spiritual growth, and our lives. If we are not growing, it is not our spouse's fault, our parents' fault, or society's fault. We have the power to change, and we must exercise it.

Work out your own salvation with fear and trembling.

—Philippians 2:12

Where are you? Do you make excuses for yourself? Do you blame your spouse or your parents? Do you say, "I can't?" Do you accept responsibility for your own emotions, or do you say, "She made me angry," or "He makes me depressed"?

RESPONSIBILITY

Always blame others	*Make excuses*	*Take some responsibility*	*Fully accept responsibility*	*Change self*

0	1	2	3	4	5	6	7	8	9	10

OPENNESS TO CHANGE

A last aspect of growth, as described by Rogers and others, is that as we grow, we become more open to new ideas, to different opinions, and to change. The person who remains closed is intolerant of others and their ideas. The man who fears change is a spiritual pygmy. Growth requires expansion. The roots must seek new sources of nourishment, and the branches must lift themselves skyward to absorb more sunlight and energy. This process is not easy. It is said that the only person who likes change is a wet baby.[9]

We must seek new challenges; we must perform new activities. As human beings, we tend to remain in what many authors call our comfort zone. We like, and we do, the things that we know we have mastered and with which we feel comfortable. We also avoid the activities that cause us anxiety and stress because they are new or uncomfortable. If we always stay within our comfort zone, however, there is no progress. The secret of personal evolution is to constantly challenge ourselves, to expand our comfort zone, to face our fears and anxieties, and to push forward. We must go beyond the limits we have created and seek higher grounds. We must become better people.

> *In a good marriage, men and women seek to improve themselves for the sake of their loved one. They offer and draw moral strength by sharing compassion, courage, honesty, , and a host of other virtues. Husband and wife complete themselves through each other, and the whole of the union becomes stronger and more wonderful than the sum of the two parts.*[10]
> —William Bennett

This is the beauty of a loving relationship. I am able to face my fears and push myself to higher levels of awareness or understanding or discipline because I have the support and encouragement of my mate. This support must be nonjudgmental, with a sincere belief and trust in my potential to accept change. This also creates a deeper and more profound relationship as each spouse expands and grows and shares their new interests and ideas with their beloved. This is the essence of being soul mates.

One measurement of this progress is our creativity. As we expand and explore new activities and ideas, we become more creative. Our fears and anxieties no longer consume our energy and we can discover or develop new talents and abilities. As we progress in awareness and concern for others, we will progressively use these new abilities and creativity to help others in our family, jobs, and social activities. Remember one of the most important titles of our Lord is that of Creator, and our purpose in life is to become similar to him and our Heavenly Father.

How open are you? Have you self-actualized and become creative in all aspects of your life? Are you constantly seeking new challenges?

OPENNESS AND ABILITY TO CHANGE

Closed	Open to some experiences	Seek new challenges	Avoid change	Some desire for change	Able to improve
0 1	2 3	4 5	6 7	8	9 10

CREATIVITY

No creativity	Some originality	Exceptionally creative
0 1 2 3	4 5 6 7	8 9 10

We measure spiritual progress in quality, not quantity. It requires balance. It is not the person who suppresses all emotions and who is over-controlled who has progressed the most but rather the person who is in control and can feel and be aware of his emotions and use them appropriately. There is a balance between rational thought and inner feelings. It is not the person who denies his own needs to serve others even when the other person abuses or uses him who is grown but rather the person who can understand his true needs, can communicate these needs, and can request the help of his mate or others. There is a healthy balance between my needs and the needs of others. It is not the person who feels responsible for everything that is wrong and who therefore is always depressed that has grown. Rather, it is the person who accepts his responsibilities and also supports the personal responsibilities of others who is spiritually stronger.

There must also be balance between the different aspects of the personality. Each human being has different dimensions such as intellectual, physical, career and finances, social, emotional, and psychological. A person who dedicates himself to just one or two spheres may progress, but there is no harmony; he remains crippled. If I am an intellectual giant but a social pygmy, I am not in equilibrium; I stunt my spiritual growth.

There are undoubtedly other aspects of spiritual growth that are more subtle and harder to chart, but if we were to achieve this much, we would be at a good point. The goal is to become a person who is completely aware and in control of his feelings and who has empathy for those of others, who is aware of his behavior and conscious and responsible for how he influences others. Someone who strives to better himself physically, intellectually, socially, and spiritually for his own growth and for the progress of those around him is mature and capable of true love. A person who develops and uses his creative energies to improve his life and the world is certainly at a higher spiritual plane. Think of the empowering effect a person like this would have in his relationships.

Once you have evaluated where you are, the questions you may have are, How do I improve myself? How do I nurture the spirit? How do I arrive at all of this?

HOW TO NURTURE THE SPIRIT

Christ wisely stated centuries ago, "Man does not live by bread alone." When was the last time you nourished your spirit? How do we go about climbing to the summit of this mountain? How do we evolve to a higher plane?

From what we said before, there are two major aspects of spiritual growth. The first is an inward journey of self-discovery, self-awareness, and self-improvement. We gain insight into our motives and learn to control our thoughts, emotions, and behaviors. Then there is an expansion of self, as we increase our awareness to others and expand our concern and empathy, moving away from selfishness to embrace those around us and all of humanity. These two aspects are not necessarily sequential. We do not have to have full self-awareness before we can experience empathy or concern for others; rather, it is a reciprocal process in which as we progress in one area it opens up understanding and awareness in other facets of growth. For example, as we enter into friendship and intimate relationships with others, this forces us to expand our concern and empathy for others. But at the same time, it also increases our self-understanding as unknown emotions or behaviors come forth and surprise us. It is a daily effort as we experience new events and ideas. We can either accept the challenge and change and grow or shut out the experience and resist change. It is up to us. Spiritual growth is a courageous choice. We have to make the decision to live, to grow, and to experience life to its fulness.

No one would climb a mountain with shackles and balls and chains attached to his feet, yet many people live this way. No eagle can soar with weights attached to its talons or with its wings clipped. These chains and weights that drag us down and impede our progress are our experiences that usually originate from childhood that we call emotional baggage. In childhood, we are particularly susceptible to the experiences, events, teachings, and discipline that we receive, and the perceptions we create will remain with us throughout life. These shape our expectations, perceptions, thinking patterns, beliefs, and attitudes, and often trigger emotional responses of fear or anger. Childhood is therefore a very important time of life.

If you visit a circus with animals, you may be surprised to find that the elephant, the most powerful animal on earth, is not held in place with heavy cords or chains. There is a simple stake driven in the ground and a thin cord attached to one leg. It is a restraint that the elephant could break in a moment by either breaking the cord or unearthing the stake, yet the elephant remains passive as soon as the cord is attached. Why? When the elephant was young, the trainer attached a heavy chain to its leg. The chain was connected to a metal or cement stake that was impossible to move. The young elephant resisted and fought the chain and tried to escape, but after a while, it learned that escape was impossible. Each time a cord was attached to that leg, the elephant became passive and no longer resisted.

Many of us are the same. We were trained and conditioned in childhood to believe that we could not perform certain tasks or did not have certain abilities. We may have learned that the world is hostile or unpredictable and developed certain fear responses or excessive aggressiveness. We were helpless as children, and those who were abused or neglected learned to remain passive or helpless.

I have the great fortune of having had a loving mother, but I remember in our family I was given the label of the intelligent child, and my sister was the creative one. It has taken decades for me to realize that I too can be creative and for my sister to know that she too is intelligent. And these were positive labels! What about all the children who are told over and over how stupid they are, how bad they are, that they were an accident and are not wanted? What emotional cords surround their legs and impede their progress? No one had perfect parents, and everyone has some conditioning and imprinting to overcome. But as the number of dysfunctional families and the number of parents who do not have time for their children increases, we will find more people with serious problems.

We are not elephants. We do not have to live our entire life conditioned by childhood experiences. Life grants us the possibility to understand many of our conflicts and to gain insight. One of the tools that life grants us to understand ourselves is forming intimate relationships. When I open up and start trusting another person, many of the issues of trust, love, and self-worth from childhood come to the surface. I become vulnerable because I am reliving some of the emotional pain that might be there from childhood. At this point, I may either shut off the emotions, keep the relationship more superficial, and never face the issues, or I gather my courage, delve in, and start understanding and facing the pain. If I have found a caring spouse, she can help me find greater self-worth and a new perception of myself and others, and to face and review my early relationship with my parents. Remember that your spouse is also facing the same task.

Jesus Christ is the great healer. He helps heal our emotional wounds in many ways. He has paid the price of our sins, and through His redeeming grace and our repentance we can lift the burden of our past errors and sins. He also teaches us to forgive. Often we must learn to forgive our parents and all those who have caused us emotional pain for their shortcomings and lack of love. This does not come easy. True forgiveness, however, allows us to unburden much of the weight that drags down our existence. The Lord can send us the Holy Ghost, who, in His function as the Comforter, can console our grief and sorrow when life's experiences become overwhelming. Most often Christ helps us heal by providing us with people and life experiences that will give us new perspectives and to teach us to love and forgive.

There is no better psychologist than a loving, caring spouse who believes in us and aids us in this process of self-awareness. We, however, must allow our spouse to be there for us. We must first open up, find trust, and allow the other person into our world. This also means that we have to be there for our spouse. This is why commitment is so important to trust. This is not an overnight process but may continue throughout most of our adult life. We can only open completely to a person who will be there for us. Each occurrence of rejection and separation demolishes part of our self-image and sets us back in our progress. Some people have to go through many relationships before they can build enough trust to finally open up. Many people never do. They remain in their shells, make sure that all their relationships are shallow and superficial, and never face the pain of feeling unloved. One of the greatest pains of life is to feel unworthy of love because your parents did not love you fully. A loving spouse can only help you overcome that pain, if you let him or her into your life.

> *The glory of friendship is not the outstretched hand, nor the kindly smile, nor the joy of companionship; it is the spiritual inspiration that comes to one when you discover that someone else believes in you and is willing to trust you with a friendship.*[11]
> —Ralph Waldo Emerson (1803–1882)

Relationships also allow us greater self-awareness because our spouse lets us see ourselves from another point of view. They see faults or defects that remain hidden to our consciousness. As long as they do this in a caring, non-critical way, we can use these insights to better understand ourselves and overcome our imperfections. Finally and most important it is the differences in our mate that most stimulate new perceptions of the world and new ways of experiencing life. It is the fact that men and women are so different that allows growth. It is because our spouse is so different that allows us to perceive the world from his or her point of view and analyze and reevaluate our own beliefs and perceptions. What greater learning process can there be?

Just as life grants us the ability to form and learn from relationships, another normal life experience that leads to great personal progress is having children. When children are born, this changes the relationship of the couple and brings forth new conflicts and emotions from their own childhoods. They gain insight into the role of parenthood and start to understand many of the conflicts that their own parents must have experienced. They find that they too are not perfect as parents, and they gain forgiveness for their parents. It may also increase their confusion about their parents as they realize that they would never do some of the things that their parents did to them.

Life forces us to see our parents as fellow human beings with many defects just like us. This means giving up our childhood myths of their superiority and perfection. We come to a new level of understanding about them and about ourselves.

Having a child also stimulates us to care for another being twenty-four hours a day, seven days a week. This teaches responsibility, commitment, caring, and concern for others in a way that no other life experience can. We learn about balancing our life and setting new priorities. We learn selflessness. As our children grow, we have the opportunity to see the world through innocent eyes, to see things creatively. Their world of perceptions is so different that it can be a humbling experience to see their insights. We must be open to that and not force them to see the world through our eyes.

Men grumble because God puts thorns with roses; wouldn't it be better to thank God that he put roses with thorns?[12]

—Anonymous

Another way that life grants us growth is through adversity. Adversity is the furnace that tempers the steel; it is the kiln that hardens the clay; it is the waterfall that erodes the rock of security and deepens the pool. All great men and women became great because they rose above life's trials and gained understanding through suffering. Look back at your life and the hardships you have faced. How have they shaped you? Would you be the same person without them? No one wants to suffer, and in the moment of adversity, we often feel overwhelmed, but it is at this moment that we learn our strengths and limits. Whether we grow with adversity or terminate our progress depends on us. The person who rebels against life or fate or God and curses their destiny does not grow. The person who realizes that all of life's trials are for their benefit obtains new insight and strengthens his soul. Embrace adversity and grow. As stated in chapter two, adversity reinforces the relationship by increasing trust and commitment.

Adversity draws men together and produces beauty and harmony in life's relationships, just as the cold of winter produces ice-flowers on the windowpanes, which vanish with the warmth.[13]

—Søren Kierkegaard

When experiences are so negative that they have distorted our perceptions or destroyed our capacity for trust, psychotherapy may be another way to gain awareness and to break the shackles that bind us to our past. The purpose of most types of therapy is to increase the self-awareness of the individual so that he can gain control over his actions and create more realistic perceptions and expectations of himself and the world around him. Therapy is another opportunity to stop and look inward and come to grips with what is pulling us down. Therapy allows us to face some of our fears and stop the constant anxiety about the future. It allows us to experience the present. Therapy is not the answer for everyone. A natural healing process within us gradually allows us to look inward and resolve many of our early conflicts. A "midlife crisis" is often the time that encourages us to stop running and look at ourselves and reevaluate who we are and what we want to achieve. The more we can listen to our souls, the more we can heal ourselves.

There are other chains and shackles that we must break before we can soar. Some of these are our bad habits. Anything that dulls our awareness or inhibits our progress drains our spirit. Alcohol and drugs dull our existential pain, but they also dull our spirit. They lower our awareness, they keep us detached from our feelings, and they become an excuse for not living to our full potential. Overeating and neglecting our bodies and our appearance does the same. Becoming a workaholic to the exclusion of family and friends or lying depressed on the couch all day are both ways to escape from the pain of living, but neither leads us up that mountain to the summit of joyful living. Escaping through TV, books, or other habits that dull our pain and our senses also erodes our joy and our sense of gratitude to the Lord for what we have. All forms of escape detract from our progress, no matter how we justify them. Look at your life. Are you living to your full potential? What could you change today? Pick one thing and start today. Spiritual growth begins with the desire to grow and the decision to make the effort.

> Some people live their lives as if they're out in the center of a big pool, treading water. They aren't making any progress in any direction. They're paddling like mad, but they're just not moving. That is the psychological plight of thousands of people. They do not go one way or the other; they just stay in the middle and feel safe. In this "safe" position they do not have to make the choices that life requires of them.
>
> But the fact is that if you stay treading water long enough in life, you're going to drown. You cannot tread water forever.[14]
>
> —Dr. Kevin Leman, *Sex Begins in the Kitchen*

It is not only emotional trauma, or conditioning experiences that represent the chains that shackle us, or the weights that we drag up the mountain of life but the choices we have made. We have to repent of the sins that we have committed. The Lord provides a beautiful description of the process of personal progress in Moroni 8:25–26:

> And the first fruits of repentance is baptism; and baptism cometh by faith unto the fulfilling the commandments; and the fulfilling of the commandments bringeth remission of sins; And the remission of sins bringeth meekness and lowliness of heart; and because of meekness and lowliness of heart cometh the visitation of the Holy Ghost, which Comforter filleth with hope and perfect love, which love endureth by diligence unto prayer, until the end shall come, when all the saints shall dwell with God.

Maybe another scale we should use is meekness and lowliness of heart. If we are not meek, we still have much repenting to do.

There are other weights that we pick up and put in our backpack that slow us down. These are the everyday clutter and worries that we have accumulated. Every time we procrastinate our responsibility, it stays in our mind and saps some of our spiritual energy. When we live in disorder, with the house a mess, and a hundred things to do that we keep putting off, each thing is like a small stone put in our pack that together weigh heavily on our soul. When you do not feel in control, you feel stress, with all its negative physical and emotional reactions. You have to change today. Liberate your soul and do those things that you have procrastinated. Pick the messiest room of the house and begin putting it in order. Continue with a different room each week. All those chores your wife has asked you to do around the house—start today and do them. As you finish each chore, feel your spirit lighten and your energy return. You have to be in control. If it is your physical appearance, vow to yourself that you will begin a new physical activity even if it is a walk around the block. Then do it. Throw away all those stones you have accumulated and lighten your load.

LISTEN TO YOUR SOUL

We need to find God, and he cannot be found in noise and restlessness. God is the friend of silence. See how nature—trees, flowers, grass— grows in silence; see the stars, the moon and the sun, how they move in silence. . . . We need silence to be able to touch souls.[15]

—Mother Teresa

How do we listen to our souls? It is not by *doing*. Rather, it is in the still, quiet moments that we tune into something more profound inside. We have to take time to meditate and ponder the events of our life. It is in these moments that we make sense of what we are doing and gain meaning from the events of our lives. These moments then fortify us to reengage in the fight for survival. A young mother who is overwhelmed with diapers, screaming children, housework, and her husband's expectations experiences only drudgery if she cannot put this into prospective. She must take some time for herself each day, not just to relax, but just to be with herself—to find meaning in what she is doing. This is not something she has to *do* but rather a moment wherein she has to *stop* doing and start feeling. The same is true for the person spending ten or twelve hours a day on building a career, returning to school, or participating in any of life's activities. He needs time to stop and evaluate each day, not to stop and watch TV or stop and read a book but to stop and look within and ask himself some questions. What have I learned today? How have I progressed? Where am I going? Am I on track? What are my priorities? Am I following them?

In a world so full of stimuli, it is difficult to stop and ponder. *Pondering* and *contemplating* are words that we hear or use rarely and are concepts foreign to our lifestyle but essential to our well-being. Turn off the TV, stop reading, and ponder. Life without TVs, stereos, and computers allows much more time for quiet meditation and intimate conversation. We must take the time to ponder. Do not just read a book, but contemplate what you are reading; mull over the concepts in your mind. Meditate about the importance of your spouse and your relationship; think deeply about the meaning of your life. This is what feeds the spirit—quiet meditation. This can be through prayer, in which not only do you tune into yourself but also into your connection with God and the universe. It can be through trained meditation, yoga, or relaxation techniques. Create a special room in your house that stimulates you to think and contemplate. It does not matter how you do it but that you take the time.

One way to gain perspective and to keep in touch with your feelings and thoughts is to keep a diary. Not only does this allow you to record your thoughts, but it also gives you a way to step outside yourself and look at life and adversity in a more abstract way. As you read through your diary, you can see how you have faced the trying moments of your life and how you have overcome them. It is a venue to express your feelings and emotions and work through your anxieties. It is a tool for spiritual growth.

Man can never be happy if he does not nourish his soul as he does his body.[16]

—The Rebbe

Think of the moments and places in your life in which you felt most at peace. Repeat those experiences. Many people find that being in touch with nature is one way to find peace and spiritual contact. A walk in the woods, a trip to the mountains or to the seashore, and gardening in the yard are all moments of spiritual contact with the world around us. Take time today to just stand and admire the sunset. Soak in the beauty of the moment and refresh your soul. Take a walk in the rain and smell the freshness of the air. Contemplate the snow and the white veil of purity that it provides. Create a special area in the yard for a flower garden or a gazebo that can be for you. Take time to live in the present and feel in touch with nature and yourself. Remember, "Man does not live by bread alone." You must feed your spirit, and you must take time to do it. If you do not take time for yourself, your personal progress, and your peace of mind, you will only feel drained, and you will have nothing to offer to your relationship or your family.

If one essential aspect of spiritual growth is to turn inward and establish a relationship with ourselves and feed our souls, then the other aspect is equally important. We must expand our capabilities, increase our abilities, and become more creative so that we can improve ourselves and those around us. First, we must have a vision of who we want to be.

Seeing yourself as you want to be is the key to personal growth

—Anonymous

One way to achieve this is to find role models. Think of someone you know and admire, someone who you believe is a spiritual giant. You may not want to start with Christ, so pick someone closer to you. You may consider people whom you know personally or historical figures who have impressed you. What qualities does this person have that you most admire? Write these down. Are these qualities part of spiritual growth? How could you develop them? How did that person develop them? Study that person's life, and search for the events or what form of discipline that person experienced or used to become that person. Study his biography. Take one aspect of his character that you most desire and create a plan on what you could do to emulate that person.

Begin today to be creative in your approach to life. The most important aspect to being creative is to believe that you are creative. Creativity starts with the search for new ways to think, to act, or to produce, but we have to decide to search. If being creative implies finding a new perspective, we have to nourish our minds with new information; we have to create new ideas. As Linus Pauling said, "The best way to get a great idea is to get many ideas."[17]

Routine kills creativity. Break your routine. If you listen to country music only, include some blues or jazz. Take a new road home from work. Try many different routes. Read different types of books or magazines. Change your hairstyle or clothing or join a new club. Do something different. You cannot stay in your comfort zone and be creative. Start a new hobby, or take up one that you have not found time for. Find the time and do it. You have to have something that you are passionate about in your life. Routine and drudgery eliminate passion. Creativity requires awareness; it requires living in the present and searching for a new future. Creativity requires us to break the shackles and weights that bind us.

If you do not know where to start in your quest for creativity, begin with your relationship. How could you change it and improve it? Take a risk and do something unexpected. Surprise your spouse. Turn off the TV and start talking about something different. Read poetry together, play charades, go to a ballet, or play some racquet ball together. Take turns deciding what new activity you can do.

Be creative with your children. Stop the toil and start playing with them. Try seeing the world from their perspective. Take some classes at a nearby college, learn photography, buy a telescope and search the skies, learn new skills. Learn a new language and then visit that country; change your life by changing yourself. There is a world of things to try and to learn, and they will enrich your life and your relationship. Start today and change something in your life.

In a garden, the best way to prevent weeds from growing is to have a healthy lawn. When we pull out a weed and leave a hole, we need to fill it with a new plant or grass or the weed will quickly return. Weeds grow in barren areas and in spots where other plants have not taken root. If we allow the weeds to become established, they quickly spread and overcome even the healthiest lawn or garden. The same is true of ourselves. Worries, anxiety, and depression take root in a barren mind or in an undernourished soul. If we pull out a bad habit, we must replace it with something positive or it will just grow again. If we are constantly tending and taking care of the garden of our soul, putting in new thoughts and habits, there is no room for depressed thoughts or constant anxiety to set in and overwhelm us. We have to take control of our lives and make it a life worth living. We have to become a person worth loving.

Many people look at the mountain and say, "It's too high; the road is too hard," and they remain in the swamps and underbrush of life. They cannot see very far and believe that this is all that life offers. Others start struggling up the side of the mountain, but they are unwilling to cast off the chains of their conditioning and the weights of their preconceptions. It takes courage to continue the journey up the slope, to strive for a better life, to struggle against our own defects and weaknesses, and to climb the mountain. It is a blessing to have a spouse who will give us a hand when they are higher up the slope and who will let us stand on their shoulders to overcome the obstacles. This is the purpose of intimate relationships—to reach the summit together, invigorated and strengthened by the journey.

NOTES

1. Alexander Solzhenitsyn. Online. *My Devotion*; available from mydevotion.com/ss/verses-00feb.asp.
2. Merriam-Webster Dictionary (New York: Simon & Schuster, 1974).
3. Gary Zukav, *The Seat of the Soul* (New York: Simon & Schuster, 1990), 165.
4. Spencer W. Kimball, *Faith Precedes the Miracle* (Salt Lake City: Deseret Book, 1973), 131.
5. William Shakespeare. Online. *Hamlet*; available from legendinc.com.
6. William R. Alger. Online. *Brainy Quotes*; available from brainyquotes.com.
7. Daniel Goleman, *Emotional Intelligence* (New York: Bantam Books, 1995).
8. David O. McKay, *Man May Know for Himself.* Claire Middlemiss, ed. (Salt Lake City: Deseret Book, 1967).
9. Roy Blitzer. Cited in Roger von Oech, *A Whack on the Side of the Head* (Stamford, Connecticut: US Games System, Inc., 1990) 28.
10. William J. Bennett, *Book of Virtues and Moral Compass.* Quoted in *Quotationary* (NovaSoft, 1999).
11. Ralph Waldo Emerson (1803–1882). Quoted in *Quotationary* (NovaSoft, 1999).
12. palikanon.com.
13. Søren Kierkegaard. Online. *Memorable Quotations;* available from memorablequotations.com.
14. Kevin Leman, *Sex Begins in the Kitchen* (Grand Rapids, Michigan: Fleming H. Revell, 1999), 194.
15. Mother Theresa of Calcutta, *In the Silence of the Heart: Meditations* (Abingdon Press, 1994).
16. Samuel Jacobson. Online. *The Wisdom of the Sages;* available from HarperCollins.com.
17. Linus Pauling. Cited in von Oech, by Roger, *A Whack on the Side of the Head* (Stamford, Connecticut: US Games System Inc., 1990), 28.

Rule 10

GROW TOGETHER

I say unto you, be one; and if ye are not one ye are not mine.
—Doctrine and Covenants 38:27

Two such as you with such a master speed
Cannot be parted nor be swept away
From one another once you are agreed
That life is only life forevermore
Together wing to wing and oar to oar.[1]

—Robert Frost

A plant in a garden seems immobile and unchanging as we observe it, but there is constant change. To live means to change. The roots of the plant are reaching downward to find new sources of water and nourishment. The leaves and flowers are growing, absorbing light from the sun, and converting it into energy. To stop this process of growth means to shrivel—to begin the process of decay and death. The same is true of each of us. We cannot remain stationary in our lives. Even if we try, the world, the people around us, and technology are all constantly changing. We are either moving forward and progressing or we lose momentum and begin to slide backwards. Either we regenerate the muscles of our body or they begin atrophy. We either use and sharpen our mental skills or they degenerate and we can no longer concentrate or reason properly. Our spirit is either growing toward the light and expanding its power or slowly closing, imploding, and becoming powerless. To live means to change; nothing remains the same.

The same is true of our relationships. Relationships are dynamic. A relationship never remains stationary but constantly evolves. We can never go back to "the way we were." We are no longer that way. As we grow or regress, we change. Our interests change, our emotions deepen, experience modifies our attitudes, and even certain aspects of our personality mutate or evolve. Just as this development occurs in us, our spouse too is changing. Not only is each member of the couple in constant flux, but the relationship too changes. The arrival of children, for example, profoundly changes the dynamics of a couple's relationship. A dyad has now become a triad, and the couple has to negotiate new responsibilities and chores and create new goals. Jealousy can emerge when we subtract time from the relationship and dedicate it to this new third party. Other life events such as a new occupation, sickness in the family, the aging or loss of parents, midlife crises, children leaving the home, or retirement all deeply impact the relationship.

As these changes occur, it is essential that we keep in contact with each other. Too often a couple comes together in great love, touches souls, and then gradually drifts apart, deadening their souls with drudgery and then separately wondering what happened to this special relationship. They often are not aware of their own development and change and do not take the time, energy, and effort to keep in contact and appreciate the evolution of their spouse. It is on the rock of routine and indifference that so many marriages shipwreck.

Can you describe how your spouse's views have changed? What new abilities or traits have they acquired? How have they deepened their understanding of life? Are you in contact with their thoughts, hopes, fantasies, and inner feelings today? Are they in contact with your thoughts, hopes, fantasies, and inner feelings today? Are you still soul mates?

Just as any building has four cornerstones and pillars that support and hold erect the whole building, so too we must build a relationship of soul mates on the four pillars of sharing time, thoughts and feelings, interests, and activities to create unity. Without any one of these, the relationship does not receive the necessary nourishment and will slowly die.

SHARE TIME TOGETHER

Time is merely the order of events, not an entity itself.[2]

—Leibnitz

Time is not an entity itself but merely a succession of events. Every day has 24 hours, 1,440 minutes, and 86,400 seconds; we decide how to use them. We order the events; we use time according to our priorities. As a result, we often use time as an excuse for ourselves and for others. When I say to you, "I would like to eat out with you, but I just do not have time," what I am really saying is, "I prefer doing other things rather than eating out with you." Alternatively, when I say to myself, "I do not exercise because I do not have time," I am really saying that I prefer to stay in bed or read a book rather than work out. These excuses are forgivable with acquaintances, but when I use them with my spouse, what am I really saying? You use time according to your priorities, and when there is never time for your spouse or your relationship, you are strongly communicating that your spouse is not high on your list of priorities.

Couples must spend time together. Soul mates need time to be with each other alone to keep in contact. Although this seems obvious and is simple, we frequently neglect it to the great detriment of the relationship. We live in a society with a frenetic pace of life. We have unrealistic expectations of what we *need* or *have* to do, and we spend our time trying to do it all. Americans and Europeans are working longer hours than ever before, and then, since work is often sedentary or stressful, we need to go to the gym and work out or go jogging. Then there is our social life, household chores, hobbies, and so on. Women are trying to do it all— trying to be the perfect wife, mother, and career woman. At the end of the day they are drained and feel miserable because they didn't manage to do everything they wanted, and tomorrow the race starts again. Where in all of this is there time for quiet meditation or for sharing thoughts and experiences of the day?

Some authors talk of the principle of reintroduction. This principle acknowledges that each of us change every day based on our experiences of that day. If we wish to keep in tune with the changes of our spouse, we must take time daily to "reintroduce" ourselves to each other to keep abreast the changes that are happening.

The saying goes, "Where there is a will there is a way." If indeed our spouse and our relationship is our number one priority, we will make the time to be there for our beloved, and our spouse will do the same for us. We have to realize the importance of having at least a half an hour a day to talk with each other—not about bills, the children, or office gossip but to open up and share our feelings or share those precious moments that have uplifted us or have stimulated reflection. Too often, when children arrive in the marriage, all conversation in the couple starts focusing around the children, and no mention is made of the couple and their relationship. You did not marry your children.

Children need your love and your energy. They are a commitment you have, but the relationship must come first. Do not forget your needs, those of your soul mate, or those of the relationship, or the children will eventually suffer the consequences of a tired and conflictual marriage. You must take time. Find time each day once the children are in bed or involved in other activities to be alone together and share your thoughts. Even without children, many couples fill their lives with so many activities that there is no room for the relationship. Decide today what your priorities are. Turn off the TV and talk, or talk about the TV programs, but open up and share your inner thoughts. If it is difficult to find time for each other. Make it a daily appointment, a fixed time for you and your spouse to be together each day. Write in your agenda "daily talk time."

Truman Madsen, in his essay "The Language of Love at Home," states the following:

> If I were newly or oldly wed, in the spring or autumn of life, I would have a time set apart every day as dependable as tropical rain when I could be in some sense really with my companion. It would be a time when we both could concentrate on nothing but each other and speak to each other sometimes in complete rapport, telegraphing the sense of being supremely important to each other. This I would make a religious ritual. The closer to worship the better.[3]

Schedule activities together. If we can schedule commitments in the workplace, why do we always forget family activities? Why can't we schedule time together? Tell the children or friends that for that half hour, they must not disturb you, and then enforce that policy. The principle is that you must have time together. This is your quality time. Make use of it. If you are not used to talking about your inner feelings, the first few times together may feel awkward with neither person knowing what to say. You may get over this initial embarrassment by finding a magazine article to read and comments or a thought for the day to discuss. Read a passage in the scriptures together and discuss it. This is not a time to focus on duties, arguments, or chores you want your spouse to do; this is time to share thoughts, experiences, and feelings. This is the time to share your spiritual intimacy.

Not only do you need a daily appointment, but you also need to continue dating, particularly when children arrive and take away from the unity of the couple. Make a date once a week. It does not have to be fancy or expensive. The best dates my wife and I have passed are evening walks when we could relax and touch spirits again. Create variety between relaxed dates and formal dates where you dress up and go out to dinner or a show. The rules are very simple:

1. You must leave home.
2. The date must last at least an hour.
3. You must go on a date weekly.
4. The date has to be enjoyable for both of you.

Dates can be continuing hobbies or activities that you both like, such as a weekly bowling night or taking a photography class together if you both enjoy that. Be aware, however, that this is time for you as a couple. This is time to feel united, so it should not be a social event with friends. You can do that too, but you need time alone. This is a time to continue courtship, to show each other that you are still in love and appreciate each other. Husbands, never take your wife for granted, and never allow her to feel that she is just part of a routine. Court her and date her, not for sex, but to show your love and appreciation. Treat her as you did before you were married; put the same intensity into courting her today as you did initially and you will see the excitement return in your relationship.

When the night you have set aside for the date arrives, you will be tired and may say to yourself or each other, "We can be together at home. Let's skip going out." You let it slide one week, then two weeks because it seems like too much an effort and things are going well anyway. However, you may soon ask yourself, "Why is my marriage going downhill?" Take the time, make the effort, pay the babysitter, and make it a habit, and you will be glad you did. David O. McKay was married for almost seventy years to his wife, Emma Rae. They never missed a Friday evening date. It was a date for her to anticipate, prepare for, and dress up for—a time of communion.

The courtship must continue throughout your life together, and this means dedicating time, energy, and special attention to your spouse each day and week. Make sure that they know that they are your number-one priority.

An added aid for couples is to get away for a romantic weekend. Find a relative or someone you trust to stay with the children, and leave your cares and worries behind. Go somewhere romantic or beautiful, or do some activity you have never done before. Be together and reestablish your unity as a couple. Be aware, however, that a weekend alone will not fix a damaged marriage. More important is talking daily or going on the weekly date. You can rarely make up in one weekend what you have been missing for years. Make being there for each other an integral part of your relationship no matter how busy you are, and the weekend will add extra spice to the relationship. The weekend alone, however, is like eating the salt and pepper without the meat!

This time together allows the couple to talk and communicate their affection and inner thoughts, which is the next pillar of the relationship.

SHARE YOUR THOUGHTS AND FEELINGS

It is impossible to *not* communicate. Every action, every gesture, what you wear, and how you appear constantly communicates something to those around you. Even the absence of words can speak loudly to your mate and to other people. If your spouse were to ask you, "Do you still love me?" your silence would be a most eloquent denial. Even a small hesitation would communicate louder than any subsequent declaration. Not writing love notes or expressing your love to your mate also communicates a negative message over time. Communication in all circumstances is both verbal and nonverbal. Studies find, however, that the more intimate the relationship is, the more important the nonverbal communication becomes. Some studies show that as much as 93 percent of what your mate receives from your message comes from the nonverbal cues. Your facial expression, the tone of your voice, your body language, and your actions communicate your true inner feelings. Any time there is a contrast between what you say and what your face, voice, and body express, your spouse will believe the latter.

Women are far better than men are at perceiving these cues. Therefore, many of the misunderstandings that occur are not about what was said but from the perceptions derived from how it was said or what was not said. For this reason, many men find that discussion and arguments are irrational and that their wife is not logical. The man wants to talk about the words and the content, and his wife wants to talk about how he said it or what he did not say. An example of this that has stuck in my mind over the years happened one morning as my wife and I woke up. We were still in bed and were looking at each other. My wife said, "You do not have that same look in your eyes that you had when you loved me." How do you argue with such a statement? I protested; I affirmed my love. I used to practice expressions in the mirror to transmit my love, but not knowing what expression "I use to have," it was hard to make it return. It was months or maybe years before Fernanda decided that I had regained the look!

Women read between the lines and fill in what was not said, and men take things at face value. Both of these positions have inherent problems. Men often hide behind the words they say, when in fact they are aware that they said it with sarcasm or hiding their true feelings. Women often read into conversation meanings that may not be there at all. It is harder to read feelings than to listen to words. Women also have the expectation that men should be able to read between the lines of their communication. What Fernanda was really trying to communicate was that our relationship was withering and she wanted it to return to where we had been. I was trying to come up with the right facial expression or create a glint in my eyes.

This leads to several conclusions. The first is that we communicate who we are and what we are feeling not only through words. If we truly want to improve the communication in our relationship, the first thing to examine is our behavior. Are we caring, sharing, and serving our mate? Do our actions reflect what we are saying? Although many marriage manuals can give good suggestions on how to better express ourselves, my experience is that if somehow trust has been betrayed because commitment and honesty are compromised, learning the right words to say is not going to heal the wound. It will only be when we regain trust by honest expression and renewed commitment that the relationship may continue. Therefore, more than learning how to say things, it is necessary to go back to the fundamental questions. Have I shown my mate that he or she is my number one priority? Are my expectations realistic? Am I blaming my spouse for my lack of spiritual growth? Am I honoring and cherishing my loved one? How have I communicated this love in a way that my spouse understands it? When you express through your actions and words that you care about your spouse, it does not matter what communication style you have or how well you are expressing yourself.

Truman Madsen has said this well:

> My notion is that the deeper thirst is not communication. It is communion. An infinity of things may remain unsaid or on the other hand said. But what is wanted—indeed needed—or else love suffocates, is the swifter and often non-verbal relationship: being in soul touch, when you are at the same depths or heights, or just in ordinary old-shoes comfort. You are aware of each other at the core. Talk alone can conceal as well as reveal . . . but not if we are in the same inward rivers together. Thus, being soul to soul even for a brief time, goes a long way.[4]

To remain in touch, to grow together, and to stay in harmony as soul mates we have to observe three fundamental principles of communication. The first is that we must continue sharing our inner thoughts and feelings and our ongoing experiences. Men in particular need to learn to become more aware of their emotions and express them. For most women this comes naturally, and they do not understand the effort that it takes men to focus in on what they are feeling and talk about it. Because of brain lateralization, for many men the only emotion that is present in their left hemisphere is anger, and they use this emotion to express all their feelings. When they are frustrated they become angry, when they feel guilty they become angry, when they are depressed they are still angry. This is wrong, and men can learn to open up and be in tune with their feelings and share them, but it takes time and effort. The wife who is patient and supportive of this effort will find that her spouse becomes more sensitive and open as time goes on. The man, however, who does not make this effort is missing an essential element of his spiritual growth and will eventually betray the trust in the relationship. We are no longer hunters who have to be strong and silent. Society has moved on, and we have to learn to interact with others and to form intimate relations. If you have a problem opening up, try this exercise.

Face your spouse and start your sentence with one of the following phrases:

> What makes me happiest deep inside is . . .
> When I was a child I . . .
> I fell in love with you because . . .
> What I like the most is when you . . .
> I had this thought about . . .
> I love you because . . .
> Right now I feel . . .
> The most important experience I have had this week is . . .

When you have finished the list, you can add your own phrases. The beauty of the exercise is that you can just start all over again because it is never ending. Consciously make the effort in the beginning to talk about how you feel. At first you may feel awkward saying these phrases, but after time it will come naturally. The level of emotional sharing of private thoughts and feelings is an indication of the trust and honesty that are present in the relationship. If you find yourself clamming up and are hesitant to share your feelings, you must look to see what has happened to the trust and commitment and address those issues.

The second principle is to pray together. As you open up your heart to the Lord, share that experience with your mate, and let her share her prayers with you. Many couples kneel holding hands, and as each pours out their heart to the Lord, their beloved is there at their side sharing this spiritual experience. Do not do this just when you are in difficulty and need the Lord's help but make it a habit of gratitude. "In every thing give thanks: for this is the will of God in Christ Jesus concerning you" (1 Thessalonians 5:18).

The third principle to learn is to listen intently to what your mate is sharing with you. Few people in our society are good listeners. It is calculated that, on average, in America we interrupt people after only fifteen to eighteen seconds. Not only this, but the more a person expresses intense emotions, the sooner we interrupt. If you also calculate that we are thinking about what we want to say before we jump in the conversation, it means that we actually listen for only a few seconds when someone is talking to us. Asian cultures consider this extremely rude, and they teach their children to not interrupt. In most Native American cultures, the listener will allow twenty or thirty seconds after the person has finished speaking before replying to make sure that they haven't interrupted the expression of the other person's thoughts. We could learn much from them. Men interrupt more quickly and more often than women do. Men cut women off in their conversations more often than they do other men. Men in general listen for facts and not for emotions.

He that answereth a matter before he heareth it (listens) it is folly and shame unto him.

—Proverbs 18:13

Try timing yourself or others the next conversation you witness. Sit back, time the conversations, and see how long each person listens to the other person before interrupting. Even better, try this exercise with your spouse. Think of a small problem you have that you can discuss with them, and ask them to do the same. Let them go first and for two minutes let them explain their problem without interrupting. You can nod, you can say, "Uh huh," but do not say anything else. Then you should talk for two minutes and they cannot interrupt. Try it. How soon do you feel the urge to jump in and make your point or to ask questions?

How difficult is it to stay quiet? When my students do this exercise in class, they are amazed at how long two minutes are. The listener usually becomes extremely frustrated, wanting to jump in. Often, there are those who just cannot stand it and interrupt with their comments anyway. Most often, they either want to ask a question or relate their own experience. For most of us, it is hard to stay silent longer than a few seconds. How often do we truly listen? The other thing that the students learn is that in relating their problem they find that after a minute or two all the emotion that was pent up regarding the problem dissipates, and frequently they find their own solution or feel better about the problem—all in two minutes! Good listening does not mean we cannot ask questions to clarify the information, but certainly, we could let people express themselves fully before we interrupt.

Even more important, however, is that men listen differently. Men tend to listen to the words and the meaning of the words but not to the underlying emotions. They are listening to gather the facts to solve the problem logically and rationally, and so they miss the most important part of the message. So even when they do listen, often they have not received the real message that their spouse wanted to communicate.

Listening is the most important part of intimate communication. Listening is another way of demonstrating that we care about what our mate has to tell us. We honor our spouse when we focus our attention on them, their ideas, and empathize with their emotions. Effective listening is a form of commitment and enhances trust; when we do not listen, we are betraying our love for our mate.

There are several steps to listening effectively.

Step 1: Pay attention—Listening while you read the newspaper or watch TV communicates clearly that you do not care or that the football game has priority. Pay attention, use eye contact, be focused on what the other person is saying and how they are saying it. You should be completely involved in what they are saying. Wives, do not pick the time of their favorite game or program to "have a talk," just to put your husbands to the test. Conversation about important subjects should wait until you both can be attentive.

Step 2: Become involved—Nodding your head, looking in their eyes, and saying "uh huh" all signal that you are attentive and listening. Ask questions that clarify what the other person is saying and let you understand the situation. This shows the other person that you are interested and are following what they are saying. A person who is involved leans toward the other and reduces personal space. This creates more intimacy and emphasizes that you care.

Step 3: Give them time to express themselves fully—Let the person talk out their problem. Wait until you can hear the emotions tone down. As people are able to express their worries or anger, their emotions diminish, and they can become more rational. Give them all the time they need and resist the impulse to jump in with your own two cents.

Step 4: Do not make judgments or offer solutions—Do not ask questions that suggest criticism, such as, "Why didn't you?" Do not offer solutions unless the person has explicitly asked for your advice. Often all you need to do is listen. It makes the person feel appreciated and in control so that they can solve their own problems. This type of active listening is so effective that for many counselors and therapists, it is the most essential element in helping the person to solve their problems.

Step 5: Give emotional and verbal feedback—Let the other person know that you have heard them. If the matter is complicated, try paraphrasing their statements to make sure that you have understood. Most important, however, is to understand their emotions and sympathize with what they are saying. Phrases like, "That must have been very stressful," or "You must have felt overwhelmed," let the person know that you understand what they went through and you have empathy. To do this, however, requires that you listen not just to the words but also to the emotional message that the person is sending. This is the most important instrument of listening. Incidentally, the word *listen* is used more than 200 times just in the Bible!

To listen effectively, you have to care about what your mate is saying and about how he or she is feeling. When you do not listen, you are communicating very strongly that you do not care.

The last principle of communication is that we need to do it more often. Remember from an earlier chapter that there needs to be a minimum of five positive affirmations of caring and appreciation for every negative expression for a relationship to work. It does not mean saying "I love you" five times a day but listening, doing something for each other, showing that you care, and supporting your mate. Do it often, and your relationship will flourish. Touch bases with each other during the day. Call your spouse at work just to say hello and hear how he or she is doing. Write those love notes that you did when you first fell in love. If you do not have the energy or time to talk in the evening, or if "he refuses to talk," write a letter and express your appreciation for your spouse, or describe your feelings. Particularly when it has been a while, sometimes it is easier to write your inner feelings and share them in writing rather than to initiate a conversation unexpectedly. It also has the benefit of leaving a permanent record of your feelings. When was the last time you wrote a love note to your mate? Do it now. Slip it in her purse or in his briefcase, or put it on your spouse's pillow. Do it now before you continue reading! Do something special to surprise your spouse.

> *I like not only to be loved but also to be told that I am loved . . . the realm of silence is large enough beyond the grave. This is the world of light and speech, and I shall take leave to tell you that you are very dear.*[5]
> —George Elliot in a letter to a friend

When was the last time you told your spouse that you cherish them and that they are dear to you? When was the last time you asked your spouse for advice? When was the last time you sought out his or her help and support? Even something as simple as opening the jar for his wife can make a man feel special and important. When we ask for advice or aid, we are showing our trust in our spouse. We communicate love. When you have an important business decision to make, discuss the problem with your spouse and seek his or her advice. Your spouse can give a new twist to the problem because even if he or she knows little about the subject matter, your spouse knows a lot about you. When you read something that touches you or interests you, discuss it and explain to your mate why it is important to you. Between soul mates, there should be a constant exchange of ideas and opinions—not necessarily agreement or consensus, but sharing our own insights and impressions.

Soul mates are not two people who think alike but two people in touch with each other's thoughts. This only comes by sharing, communicating, and listening to one another.

SHARED INTERESTS

In the difficult balance between belonging and independence, between intimacy and separation, it is necessary that both occur. Each individual in a couple needs personal space to develop and grow, and it is healthy for them to independently pursue their personal interests. On the other hand, it is equally important that the couple have time together to communicate and to share common activities and hobbies. The husband who, after the work week leaves the family every weekend to pursue scuba diving or mountain climbing or whatever, is neglecting his wife. The wife who is too involved in the children's schoolwork or activities and does not have time to be with her husband is equally neglectful. Remember that common interests were one of the major attractions that created the relationship in the beginning. Think back to your courtship and early marriage. How much time did you spend together? What did you do together? Are you still doing it?

In a team, each player can exhibit and use his individual talents, but there has to be teamwork, interplay, and passing, or there is no team. In a business relationship, each person can have different responsibilities, but there has to be sharing of information, similar goals, and a similar passion for the business or there is no synergy.

What unites you and your spouse are your common goals and interests. Share your passions; teach each other. Fernanda came from a long line of farmers and inherited their love for the land. She has shared this with me, teaching me each aspect of caring for fruit trees, vegetables, and flowers. We spend many weekends in spring in the garden digging, fertilizing, and planting. Sometimes my contribution is nothing more than to sit in the sun and watch her, giving my precious oversight! We now share a common love. Her passion has become our passion.

I love basketball. My concept of heaven is playing basketball twenty-four hours a day. I have played with all three of my sons who have all surpassed my scarce abilities. Each Saturday, if the weather cooperates, we still play together for a couple of hours on the court. Fernanda knew little about basketball. She still does not play, but she has learned all the nuances of the game. She recognizes the stars of the NBA and sometimes we watch games together. Over the years, we have attended together hundreds of our sons' games, and she is a strong fan. We yell at the referees together and share the triumphs and defeats of our sons. My passion has become our passion.

We share a love for nature and the mountains and for good literature. We both like to read, but we read different types of books. She likes historical novels and I like thrillers. We both like music, but she likes R&B and I like rock. She has influenced me to appreciate Aretha Franklin and Otis Redding, and I have persuaded her of the merits of Eric Clapton and Carlos Santana. It is not necessary or healthy to be the same or to share all interests, but there have to be points of encounter. Otherwise, the spouses start living separate lives and drift apart. At times, it takes effort to share each other's passions. My wife could have ignored or belittled my love for basketball, and eventually instead of it being something that unites us, it would've become a factor for disunity and separation.

What are the passions and interests of your spouse? Try listing your spouse's top five.

Passions or interests of my spouse:
1.

2.

3.

4.

5.

What are your passions and interests? List your top five.
1.

2.

3.

4.

5.

What interests and passions do you share and do together?
1.

2.

3.

4.

5.

If there is nothing on this list, something is wrong. Go back to the previous lists and ask yourself which of your mate's interests or passions you could share. What aspect of your spouse's life would you like to share? Then look at your list and ask yourself, "What could I share with my spouse?" Ask yourself, "Are there new interests that we could develop and share together?" Talk together and plan activities or hobbies that you could share as a couple. If the only thing that is keeping you together is the children, eventually that will not be enough.

To be a couple, to be soul mates, you must have unity of purpose and a meeting of the minds. But this does not come easily.

CREATE UNITY

The dictionary defines unity as "the quality or state of being one. Concord, accord, and harmony. Continuity without change as in unity of purpose."[6] As we have described, there has to be a unity of purpose in pursuing life goals as a couple. It has been said, "United we stand, divided we fall."[7] This is certainly true of marriage. In the history of the world, all the major empires have fallen to external conquest only after they have been weakened by internal strife. A person who unites with friends, other family members including children, or other people outside the relationship to criticize their spouse has broken the unity of the couple and betrayed their spouse. There has to be harmony and accord or the relationship will become a battleground. Even more, the relationship should be a safe haven against the storms of life. We should find refuge and protection with our beloved against a hostile world. We have repeatedly stated that adversity can strengthen the bonds of the relationship because this gives us the opportunity to show our love and support. This is only true, however, when the two people remain united against the difficulties that life offers. United we must stand because it is better to be alone than to have your beloved attack you from behind.

When spider webs unite, they can tie up a lion.

—Ethiopian proverb

Unity, however, does not mean that we do everything in the same way. Many people have a false expectation of unity as the total fusion of two people into one harmonious couple. Their idea is that we start the relationship as two people and then slowly blend into one. This unit of the couple should think alike, do everything together, and never argue. This is their image of the perfect couple and they are then repeatedly disappointed when they discover the vast differences that separate them from their spouse. They wrongly take these differences as evidence that they were unable to unite and therefore there is no true love. This concept of love and unity is more similar to that of the ivy that tightly clings and adorns the oak tree. It is beautiful to watch, particularly in the fall with the splendid contrast in colors, but underneath the facade, the ivy is slowly strangling the tree, sucking the lymph that sustains it.

> But let there be spaces in your togetherness,
> And let the winds of the heavens dance between you.
> Love one another, but make not a bond of love:
> Let it rather be a moving sea between the shores of your souls.
> Give your hearts, but not into each other's keeping.
> For only the hand of Life can contain your hearts.
> And stand together yet not too near together;
> For the pillars of the temple stand apart,
> And the oak tree and the cypress grow not in each other's shadow.[8]
> —Kahil Gibrain, *The Prophet*

A couple is two separate plants that choose to grow together to enhance one another. They intertwine and exalt each other, but they remain separate plants. The couple is similar to two dancers that follow the same rhythm and move in tandem but also separate to show their particular talents. They remain in touch, and they come together again. They have a perfect unity of purpose and they feel and anticipate each other's moves, but they are both free to express their abilities. They separate, remain in touch by no more than a finger or hand, move to the music, and reunite. In a relationship, it is necessary for there to be space for individual growth, but this can only occur if there are periods of intense belonging. This follows the pattern of growth throughout life. The young infant is completely dependent on his mother. He attaches and bonds both physically and emotionally with his mother. Then, however, for the infant to develop, he must separate and become independent and autonomous. What psychology and experience teach us is that there are two necessary aspects to this kind of growth. First, there must be a period of belonging, and then there must be space for separation. Thus, the infant who has difficulty in his attachment because the primary care giver is unable or uninterested in properly taking care of his needs has never belonged, and is the toddler that has the most problems separating and developing. To allow the growth of the infant requires that first we love him unconditionally, taking care of all his needs, and then we allow space for the child to try out his new skills and qualities. The infant has learned to trust his caregiver and knows that she will meet his needs, so he is able to break away and explore his environment. He is able to assert his own personality. He is able to say "no" to Mother because he knows that she will still love him. There is now tension because the caregiver has to adjust to the needs and desires of the toddler. She is no longer in complete control, and so where there was harmony there is now tension and argument—the terrible twos. This, however, is sign of love and growth, not the opposite.

Whereas some parents are incapable or only partially capable of taking care of the emotional and physical needs of the child, others become so attached to the child that they are like the ivy, and they strangle the growth of their child's young spirit. They are over protective and won't let the child experiment and explore on his own because they "love" him too much and do not want him to be hurt. There must be space for separation. Nature's pattern is, first, we belong and then we separate. The same process occurs again in adolescence. The developing child needs to separate emotionally from his family. The child who feels part of the family and who receives space to grow and experiment can properly make this transition. This adolescent finds more rapidly his own identity. The child who still has strong needs for affection that have not been satisfied is the one who will have difficulty growing and adjusting. Again, there are parents ready to push the child away before his belonging and emotional needs have been satisfied, and those who control and cling and stunt the developmental process.

In a relationship, this same process continues. We first meet, belong intensely, lower our barriers, and create intimacy. We need to feel the emotional support and nourishment to continue our growth. We touch minds and touch spirits. Then it seems that we move apart, and some people wrongly view this as frightening and threatening, so they cling and try to control. This distorts the relationship from its natural process and creates negative tension and conflict that may end up destroying the couple. It is because we need to have times of independence that it is so important to create the love, trust, and commitment early in the spouseship. Just as the trusting child will explore the environment on his own but then run to Mom with his new discoveries or needs, so each spouse can explore and experience life in their own way but then come and share these experiences with their beloved.

After a period of intense emotional sharing or physical intimacy, many couples may find themselves bickering or grumbling for no good reason. Unconsciously, maybe they realize that they are uncomfortable with the closeness they have created and they seek distance. Not knowing how to request it, or still living in the myth that they are *supposed* to always feel close, they use arguments, anger, or coldness to separate. Their spouse is left wondering what happened. "We were so close. Why is he acting like he hates me?" is a question many wives ask themselves. If we understand that this ebb and flow is a natural process, we can find safer and more effective ways to take and allow separation. As Gay and Kathlyn Hendricks state in their book *Conscious Living, The Journey to Co-Commitment,*

> You would not think of working all day without sleeping at night. Neither would you think of eating a big meal without giving yourself time to digest before eating another one. Intimacy works the same way. You need those times of solitude in order to integrate the powerful energy of closeness. By resting between each energetic dance, you are ready next time to take the floor at a new and higher level.[9]

It is inevitable that sometimes one spouse needs closeness while the other is seeking solitude. We have to be careful that even while we are separate, making our own pirouettes, that we are still available to provide for the emotional needs of our spouse—that we are able to snap back into the rhythm of the music and the embrace of our loved one. Just as we do not allow a child to play in the street, there are limits to the emotional space we can and should create. Love is founded on trust, and we never betray that trust without severely damaging the relationship. We can never become so involved in our own steps and movements that we forget that we are together in this dance of love and life. A particularly difficult time in life for relationships is the period of midlife when both spouses seek space to reevaluate their lives.

It is not by chance that divorces mostly occur either early in the relationship or years later after the children grow up and the parents enter their mid-life crises. This is a time in life around forty to forty-five for men and at about age thirty-five for women, when we start questioning the choices we have made and reevaluate our priorities. Even in the best relationships, it can be a difficult time as each spouse is seeking space to turn inward, but at the same time needs emotional support and love from their spouse. When a relationship has been languishing and has lapsed into indifference, or the couple is engaged in constant conflict, one or both spouses may feel that the relationship should terminate. The idea is that this is the last chance they have to find love and romance before they are too old to attract a spouse. Frequently, they blame their own lack of happiness or spiritual growth on their spouse and think that with a new spouse it will be different.

Instead, if we use this period of life properly, it can be a positive, invigorating experience in which we find out what is really important, establish contact with our soul and our deep and true feelings, and create new goals and priorities. We can invest in our relationship with new energy because we realize that our mate and family are in fact the most important element of our growth, and we can create a deeper and more meaningful relationship. Now, we are ready and able to truly touch spirits and become soul mates. Almost all couples who work through this difficult period find that their relationship improves immensely, gaining deeper meaning and spiritual sharing. They become truly united.

No one would confuse the two dancers as being just two individuals on the floor each doing their own dance. They are two separate individuals united in their purpose, who move to the same rhythm and who have coordinated each movement. They form a couple, and the greater their synchronized movements as they embrace and separate, the more beautiful the dance. In the truly great dancers or figure skaters, you can feel their perfect harmonization from hours of practice; they know exactly what to expect from each other. They have reached a near perfect union. So it is with the couple, as each allows the other to separate and practice their moves. They learn just when to re-embrace and continue the dance together. They are in harmony, synchronized, and united.

These are the four cornerstones of the foundation as a couple: You must spend time together to communicate affection, love, and appreciation for each other. You must learn to listen, not just to the words but also to the feelings of your spouse and validate those feelings. You must share interests together, and you must find unity as a couple, and each person must grow spiritually, intellectually, socially, and physically, stimulated by the trust and encouragement of their spouse. But they must share these experiences with each other. They cannot remain separate experiences or they will divide the couple. When the couple shares them, then they can grow together, and reach a deeper level and communicate soul to soul. In the words of George Eliot: "What greater thing is there for two human souls than to feel that they are joined to strengthen each other, to be at one with each other in silent unspeakable memories."[10]

Each plant now is healthy and flowers vigorously, and together they form a perfection of contrast and add beauty to the garden. They are in total symbiosis, each adding to the well being of the other and giving delight and appreciation to their family and others. No couple starts like this. We must earn and show trust through the school of life and its adversities. Patience, unconditional love, and putting our mate's needs first are virtues that we learn as we progress. We must always examine first our own fantasies and unrealistic expectations before we can blame our spouse. Often this means going through the painful experience of shedding the weights of our emotional baggage. We must first discover and then value the differences between us so that they will unite us and not separate us as a couple. We must grow spiritually and we must support the growth of our mate so that we can climb higher up the mountain of life. We must have the same goals and values, we must be climbing the same mountain, and we must do it together. The one who is further along in his progress must stop and give a hand to his spouse so they can reach the peak together. The promise is that from the height of the mountain peak, the world is beautiful, and we can share this profound joy and meaning with the person we love most—our soul mate. We can share this unity together for all eternity with our celestial soul mate.

1. Robert Frost, "The Master Speed," inscribed on the gravestone of Frost and his wife, Elinor.
2. "Leibniz's Philosophy of the Mind." Online. *Stanford Encyclopedia of Philosophy*; available from plato.stanford.edu/entries/leibniz-mind/.
3. Truman Madsen, *Four Essays on Love* (Provo, Utah: Communications Workshop, 1971), 51.
4. Ibid.
5. George Eliot and A.S. Byatt, *Selected Essays, Poems and Other Writings*. Nicholas Warren, ed. (Penguin Classics, 1991).
6. Merriam-Webster Dictionary (New York: Simon & Schuster, 1974).
7. John Dicksenson. Online. "Liberty Song," 1768, Wikipedia Encyclopedia; available from www.wikipedia.org.
8. Kahil Gibran, *The Prophet* (New York: Alfred A. Knolpf, 1967), 12–15.
9. Gay and Kathlyn Hendricks, PhDs, *Conscious Loving: The Journey to Co-Commitment* (New York: Bantam Books, 1992).
10. George Eliot. Online. Quoted from *My Quotation Page, Laura Moncur's Motivation Quotes* n. 37949; available from www.myquotationpage.com.

Index

About the Author

Trafford R. Cole is a clinical psychologist. He graduated from Padua University in Italy in 1982, and did post-graduate training in marriage counseling and sex therapy. After several years of private practice, he began teaching psychology courses for the European division of the University of Maryland. He has taught U.S. military members and dependents at several bases in Northern Italy for the last twenty years. He enriched his experience by working for several years for the Army Family Advocacy Program as an educator teaching courses on parenting, relationship enrichment, stress management, and child abuse recognition.

He has also worked as a professional genealogist for Italy and has written numerous articles on the topic. His book *Italian Genealogical Records* has remained a classic in the field of Italian genealogy.

He presently lives in Italy with his wife, Fernanda, and his three sons, Joel, Jeffrey, and Jason.